FOLK TALES *of* TIBET

NORBU CHOPHEL

LIBRARY OF TIBETAN WORKS & ARCHIVES

First Print 1984
Reprints 1989, 1993, 2000
This Edition 2010

ISBN: 978-93-80359-19-9

Published by the Library of Tibetan Works and Archives, Dharamsala, H.P. 176215, and printed at Indraprastha Press (CBT), Nehru House, New Delhi-110002

Contents

Dedicated to my sponsor, Miss R.G. Makkink of Deventer, Holland, and to my parents.

Publisher's Note

TIBETAN FOLK TALES, compiled and written by Norbu Chophel, is yet another attempt in LTWA's continuing efforts for the preservation and dissemination of Tibet's rich oral folk literature. The necessity for this effort arises since many of the oral folk traditions are fast disappearing.

Norbu Chophel collected and translated materials for this work spread over several years, beginning in late 1977. The work is presented in simple, straightforward language keeping as close as possible to the original flavour of the oral narration.

It was first published in 1984 and reprinted three times since then. We hope this revised edition will gladden the hearts of both young and old. We would like to thank Ms. Katrina Moxey from Australia for editing this revised edition.

Publication Department
LTWA
2010

Preface

Story-telling in Tibet occupied a very important place, being one of the main sources of recreation. In the evenings grandmothers or grandfathers told endless folk stories while the rest of the family sat by the fireside listening to them. The aged shared their stories with the younger generation and so helped pass down this oral tradition.

There were also professional story-tellers who earned their livelihood by telling stories. Some of them specialised in folk stories, some in the *Gesar* epic, while others, called *Lama-manis* (a sort of minstrel or bard), told stories about *Dharma** and hell. They did not ask a fee but were offered something in return for their efforts.

Gesar epic stories do not contain anything sentimental to arouse the emotions and provoke sympathetic tears. These stories are full of battles and bravery. Ordinary folk tales, as in the folk stories of other civilisations, do sometimes arouse one's emotions and the stories that a *Lama-mani* tells are full of sadness and do so easily. People sit for hours at a stretch listening to him, wiping away their tears and then going home with red eyes.

Times have changed now: but for fewer than half a dozen *Lama-manis,* there is not a single professional story-teller actively recounting the legendary *Gesar* epic or the ordinary folk tales. These traditions are dead.

In an attempt to restore and preserve these traditions for posterity, the Library of Tibetan Works & Archives has made a substantial effort

---

* See glossary at the end for all non-English words

in recording the recitations of two prominent *Lama-manis.* It is also publishing serialised works on the different stories of the *Gesar* epic in Tibetan, and has already published two books on Tibetan folk tales, one in Tibetan and one in English.

As my own small contribution to the preservation of Tibetan folk tales, I have collected a few stories in the Tibetan settlement at Mundgod. Only a few, yes, because most of the people I talked to or requested stories from, either said that they had forgotten them completely or could not remember them properly. That's the sad part of the matter.

Although I would not claim that the stories that I have translated are the purest form of transltation, I have taken the utmost care to see that they are presented in their closest form and that the translations are as faithful as possible. Some books in English on Tibetan folk tales do no more than inform us that such a tradition existed and still persists. The translators have employed so much of their own imagination and epigrammatical construction in between the main parts of the stories, that it has resulted in a deviation from the general style of the tradition of Tibetan folk tales. Of course, a little imagination can reasonably be introduced to make the stories lively, but beyond that is a gross violation of the Tibetan tradition. For instance, no Tibetan story-teller would go to the extent of describing the scenery in its minutest detail before proceeding with the main story; they would simply say that it was a beautiful valley, place or hill, but never beyond that (maybe the Tibetans have no aesthetic sense!).

Difference in culture renders a thoroughly accurate translation impossible. Many Tibetan words have been retained in phonetic transliteration, because translating or substituting English words for them would make the stories a jumble of words, which would destroy their flavour.

Anyway, I hope readers will enjoy the stories and have dreams of travelling to the Kingdom of the Dragons.

Finally, I am indebted to all those who spent their time telling me stories including my mother and uncle; to Mr. Tashi Tsering Josayma for the three stories that he contributed from his own collection; Mr.

Tashi (Broger) for taking his time to tell me two long stories; the Director of this Library, Mr. Gyatsho Tshering, and Mr. K. Dhondup and all those who gave me encouragement; Mr. Jeremy Russell for going through the entire manuscript and suggesting improvements; Mr. Lobsang Gedun for doing the illustrations within such a short time, and Mr. Nyaljor Samten for supervising and giving ideas on the illustrations. To all I am grateful because this book is not the outcome of my own efforts alone but the result of their contributions and efforts too.

Dharamsala
September 1983

The Three Sisters

Not very far from a place called Potala there lived a couple who had three beautiful daughters. They were a very happy family. As the years went by the fame of the girls' beauty spread far and wide. Many young and handsome men sought them to be their brides, but were either refused by the parents or rejected by the girls. The beauty of the girls was so striking, that whenever they went out of their house, they stole the glances and hearts of all. Thus, they were seldom allowed to go out, because the parents feared that something dreadful might happen to them.

Every year a great fun-fair was held at Potala, which the three sisters had never attended, because their parents had never allowed them to go. But one year, when they begged their parents' permission and promised that they would behave well and return home before dark, they were allowed to go. Gleaming with joy and excitement they dressed themselves in their best *chupas* and put on their most expensive jewellery. Each compared herself with the other two to see if she herself looked better and more beautiful than the others. All of them looked immaculate and beautiful in their festive attire, but the middle sister whose name was Dhampa Khechog possessed all the fine qualities of a perfect and matchless beauty.

At the fun-fair each went her own way. They were determined to make the best use of that single precious day. They had a lovely time playing, being admired by the crowd and watching other people in their colourful dresses. Indeed, they had such a delightful time that they forgot that it was already getting dark. Without waiting or looking for Dhampa Khechog, the other two sisters returned home and told tales of her bad behaviour and that she had flirted with many men.

Angered by Dhampa Khechog's antics, her parents did not even allow her to step into the house when she returned home the next morning. She tried to explain to them that it was not her fault that she had been unable to return with the other two sisters, because she had been kidnapped. But her sisters' words had been more powerful than her pleading and confession and she was sent away with nothing but a torn *chupa*, a broken sickle and a broken pitcher.

With nothing to eat she could not go far, so she went to Potala and sat on the steps of the *zongpon's* house. People passing by looked twice at her but, somehow, were too proud to ask anything of her. However, the *zongpon* was an amiable man with no pride. After hearing her story he called her inside, dressed her in a *chupa* made of brocade and bought her expensive jewellery of gold, silver and turquoise. He then married her without thinking twice or asking her any questions. He invited all the people of the village and celebrated with great pomp and show for seven days and seven nights.

For many years she lived happily and comfortably with the *zongpon,* with all the luxuries of the world. The magistrate loved her and treated her very kindly. He took her wherever she wanted to go and gave her whatever she asked for. With a number of servants to herself she did not have to do any work. Amidst all the luxuries and comforts of the world, the attention that she received from the *zongpon* and the number of servants she had, she was no less than a queen of a powerful kingdom. She was very happy there.

But, as time went on, she gradually lost her taste for wealth and idle happiness and sympathised very much with her parents and two sisters, who were not fortunate enough to enjoy the comforts of life as she did. She always thought of them and wanted to meet and help them.

One day she took the *zongpon* onto the terrace of their house and said to him, "I am very happy with you, but there across the valley live my poor and aged parents and two sisters. I haven't seen them since I came here and now I long to meet them. Please allow me to go."

Kind-hearted as he was, he not only agreed to her simple request, he even gave her presents to take home. He went to his store-house and weighed out the solid turquoise and measure the pieces into a *bo*; he weighed out solid gold and measured the smaller pieces, and he did likewise with onyx and ruby. He had them loaded onto a caravan of horses and sent her off to see her parents and sisters with an entourage and several guards.

Seeing so many people coming in the direction of their house, the mother sent her eldest daughter to receive the party with *chemar* in her right hand and a bowl of *chang* in her left. When she saw Dhampa Khechog, the elder daughter sang:

"Listen to me once, Dhampa Khechog Bhuti,
With such dress and jewellery
You don't look like our Khechog Bhuti,
But the look of your face shows you are our,
Khechog Bhuti."

Without offering the *chemar* or the *chang* she went home and told her parents that the girl she went to receive was not their Dhampa Khechog Bhuti but some other rich lady.

Then the mother sent the youngest daughter to receive the party with *chemar* in her right hand and a bowl of *chang* in her left. She also sang:

"Listen to me once sister, Dhampa Khechog Bhuti
With that dress and jewellery
You don't look like our Khechog Bhuti,
But the look of your face shows you are our
Khechog Bhuti,
If you are our Khechog Bhuti,
Please accept the *chemar* and *chang*."

Dhampa Khechog Bhuti immediately accepted the *chemar* and *chang* and tossed a little from both heavenward, praying for a happy reunion. They became very happy on recognising each other and flung themselves into an affectionate embrace. Hand in hand and with tears of joy they went home together. The parents also wept with joy at the very sight of their long lost, middle daughter. All of them begged Dhampa Khechog Bhuti's forgiveness for what they had done to her many years before.

Then the horses were unloaded and the wealth overfilled the house. The once poor home became the object of envy of the other villagers. Then for seven times three, twenty-one days there was a great feast for all the people of the village. It was a happy reunion and an occasion for great rejoicing.

Happiness with rejoicing,
Rejoicing and prosperity.

The Song of the Little Dog

Many hundreds of years ago there was a mother who had three daughters. Every day one of the daughters went to graze their small herd of *yaks* and *dzos*. One day, one of the *dzos* deserted the herd and could not be found.

On the following day the mother packed some *tsampa* in a *thangkuk* and sent the eldest daughter to look for the *dzo*. She searched for a long time, but could not find the *dzo*. When night fell she came upon an old cottage and decided to spend the night there. She knocked on the door and an old woman opened it and generously offered her food and shelter. The old woman was a witch and had a little dog, whom she mostly allowed to starve. When the girl was eating her *pak*, the hungry little dog came to her and sang:

"Give me one handful of *pak*,
And I will tell you a sweet word.
Give me two handfulls of *pak*,
And I will tell you two sweet words."

But the girl was very hard-hearted and thought that a dog could tell her nothing nice, so she angrily shooed it away. Being hungry herself, she ate all the *pak* and went to sleep on the lower bunk, while the witch slept on the upper bunk,

In the middle of the night the old witch got up, killed the girl by smashing a big pot on her head, and used her brain and intestines to brew her magic potion.

The next day, when the elder daughter did not return, the mother sent the second daughter in search of the *dzo*. But she too met the same fate at the hands of the old witch.

On the third day, when her sisters did not return home, the youngest daughter begged her mother to allow her to go in search of the *dzo* and her sisters. Just as she had done for the other two daughters, the mother put some *tsampa* in a *thangkuk* and sent her youngest daughter in search of the sisters and the *dzo*.

She searched in every direction, crossed rivers and valleys, climbed hills and mountains, but could not find the *dzo* nor her sisters. It was already getting dark and she was quite exhausted and far away from home, so she sat under a tree to rest and night fell quickly. Everywhere was dark and she had an eerie feeling of being watched and became very frightened.

In the distance she saw a small light and going in that direction she came to an old cottage. She knocked on the door and the old witch opened it to her with a great show of sympathy. The witch gave her tea, food and every hospitality she could afford. Just as it had done before, the little dog went to the girl and sang:

"Give me one handful of *pak*,
And I will tell you a sweet word.
Give me two handfulls of *pak*,
And I will tell you two sweet words."

Unlike her two sisters, she was very kind-hearted and gave the little dog two handfulls of *pak*. The little dog ate them hungrily and said, "For your kindness I have a few words of advice to give you: when the old witch asks you 'where do you want to sleep?' tell her that you want to sleep with me. Your two sisters were unkind and did not listen to my words, and the old witch killed them. You should also get up very early in the morning and run away as fast as you can. If she chases you, throw a needle for it will multiply at once and will prick her feet, so she will be unable to catch and kill you."

When it was time to sleep, the old witch asked her, "Where do you want to sleep, my dear girl?"

"I want to sleep with the dog," replied the girl, remembering the little dog's advice.

The old witch insisted that human beings should not sleep with dogs and that being her special guest for the night, she should sleep on her specially prepared bed. But the girl was adamant and slept with the dog.

The next morning the girl got up early and ran away. When the witch found her missing, she blazed with anger and at once set out in pursuit of the girl. As the witch came near, the girl dropped a needle behind her, which multiplied and pricked the witch's feet. While the witch was busy pulling them out, she was able to gain some distance. But the witch had no sooner picked out the needles, than she caught up with the girl. So the girl threw thorns on the path, which also multiplied and pricked the witch's feet. And while the witch was plucking the thorns out of her feet, the girl reached her home and shouted from the courtyard:

> "Dear mother, the unbreakable iron,
> Or the breakable woollen rope!"

The mother dropped down one end of the iron chain and the girl climbed to safety. Then came the witch who called like the girl, but she was thrown the woollen rope. When she was half-way up it, the rope snapped and the old witch fell down and died. That was the end of the ugly old witch.

The Adventures of a Minister's Son

In the beginning there lived a powerful King whose fame spread far and wide, to all corners of the world. He had seven external ministers, seven internal ministers and seven common ministers—a total of twenty-one ministers in all.

Not all the ministers were good. One of them by the name of Kala Yulchan kept more power for himself. He often bullied the other, meeker ministers and servants and was always jealous and angry with them. But the other ministers were simple, honest and unambitious, they did not fight for power nor raise any word of revolt against Kala Yulchan. They were all afraid of his dictatorial commands, which they feared more than the King's orders.

Once, for no apparent reason, Kala Yulchan developed a personal dislike for one of the meeker ministers. He ousted the minister from his post and sent his wife and son to look after the fearful, red ox. The poor minister had no option but to obey and the mother and son went to look after the red ox. Sometimes the mother went alone, sometimes the son went alone and at other times they went together. Whenever they went together the mother told her son stories that she knew. She also told him not to worry about their new life and comforted her son with the assurance that it was only a passage to a brighter future for them.

One day, when he was alone with the red ox, the son saw a thumb-sized wizard taking away the Queen. He shooed and booed and hurled his axe at the wizard with all the force of his small hands, but the wizard escaped with the Queen and disappeared under the ground.

When the King found his Queen missing, he assembled all his people and asked if any of them had seen her. He promised to reward the person who brought the Queen back to him with half of his kingdom. The boy went to the King and said that he had seen a wizard taking the Queen away and that he would need a hundred men, a hundred ropes, a hundred needles and a hundred pieces of thread to rescue her. The King immediately ordered his ministers to bring what the boy had asked for and to recruit a hundred strong men, who were then handed over to the boy.

The boy wasted no time, to each man he gave a needle and a piece of thread and asked them to stitch the hundred ropes together. Then he went to the place where the wizard had entered the ground. It was a huge, deep cave that seemed to have no end. He tied one end of the rope to his waist and instructed the hundred men to pull the rope, when he gave the signal by pulling it three times and went down into the cave.

He went deep down into the cave until the entire length of the rope was finished, so he tied the end to a rock and went searching for the Queen. Just then, he found himself inside a well-lit area, which was the wizard's kitchen. In one big pot was rice and soup in another. The wizard's dinner was ready. Soon a ladle came floating through the air from nowhere, followed by four big bowls. Though the wizard was nowhere in sight the ladle poured rice into two bowls and soup into the other two. After that the bowls floated away through the air and he followed them cautiously.

He came to another well-lit room littered with heaps of human and animal bones. He thought that the wizard might have already eaten the Queen, but when two bowls floated towards a dark corner he found the queen, almost unconscious with fright and worry. He told her that he was the son of the minister ousted by Kala Yulchan and that he had come to rescue her. He asked her where the wizard was and she pointed him in the direction and told him to follow the other two bowls. He did so, and soon came to where the wizard was, then swinging his axe at the wizard's head, he killed him swiftly.

In a remote corner of the cave he met the wizard's shepherd and asked him if there were any other wizards or human beings in the cave. The shepherd told him that except for the Prince of the Dragon World, there were no other living beings in the cave. So he went in search of the Prince of the Dragon World and found him lying half dead in another remote corner of the huge cave. Immediately, he went to the wizard's kitchen and fetched food for the Prince.

He then decided to get out of the cave with the queen and the Prince as soon as possible. He tied the rope around the Queen's waist and pulled it three times. The men waiting at the mouth of the cave pulled the Queen up, but did not drop the rope down again for the boy. They had already entered into a conspiracy to leave the boy inside the cave to die, because they feared that the King would punish them for failing to rescue the Queen. They had decided to tell lies to the King and earn the reward for themselves and had even threatened and persuaded the Queen to say that they were the ones who rescued her and not the boy. When they reached the palace, they told the King stories of the danger and difficulties they had faced in rescuing the Queen. The King was greatly pleased and rewarded them with half of his kingdom.

Meanwhile, the boy and the Prince of the Dragon World became very good friends and remained a long time in the cave. They wandered from one room to another, but everywhere they went they found nothing but bones.

One day when the Prince of the Dragon World felt healthy enough, he put the boy under his wing and flew off with him to his own kingdom. There the King, Queen and the whole kingdom wept with joy at the return of their only Prince and feasted for days on end. The boy was given a richly furnished room to live in, was offered the best food of the kingdom and was entertained by the dances of the kingdom's most beautiful boys and girls. He was so happy that he forgot how and why he was there in that strange land and almost forgot even his parents and his own country.

Every day he dropped a little of his food into a hole, from which he could hear the faint moaning of a man, but was unable to discover who was underneath. This went on for several days until, one day, he was taken around the palace to see the Dragon's wealth. While he was being shown from one room to another, from one sumptuous chamber to another, he came upon a door with a rusted lock on it and asked the Prince, "What is in this chamber?"

"There is nothing worth seeing in this room," said the Prince. "Our baby-sitter was locked up here thirty years ago, when he lost me, with only three bags of rice to eat. It has been such a long time, that only his dead body must be left and there is no use looking at a crumbling corpse."

"I am grateful to you for showing me around your great and lovely palace. Now, as a favour, I request you to open the rusted lock and let me peek into the room."

The Prince opened the lock and inside they found the baby-sitter still alive. The Prince was very surprised that he had survived three long years of confinement. The boy begged the Prince to release the man and promised to ask for no more favours. The grateful baby-sitter got slowly to his feet, bowed low before the Prince and thanking the boy, went away, staggering to freedom.

One day when the boy was alone, the baby-sitter snuck quietly into his room and said, "The Prince will ask you what you want in return for saving his life. You must ask only for the black and the white vases. This is the only favour I can offer, in return for saving my life. If you had not dropped food through that hole, I would surely be dead by now."

After staying in the Dragon Kingdom for many more days he went to the Prince and told him that he wanted to go back to his parents and his own land.

"Please stay with us for a few days more," begged the Prince. "What makes you so unhappy here, that you want to leave us so quickly?"

The boy replied that he was very happy and thanked him for all the hospitality, but he said, "I have stayed here long enough and now I wish to go back to my own land. It is not because I am unhappy here that I want to leave you, but because of my desire to see my poor and ageing parents."

Further persuasion was to no avail and finally the Prince said, "For rescuing me from the wizard I will give you anything you wish out of my wealth."

The boy then remembered what the baby-sitter had advised him and asked for the black and the white vases. The Prince wondered if these were the only things he needed, "Why not some gems and other precious stones?" he asked.

"I would be quite content with the vases," the boy replied.

The Prince then put the boy with the vases under his wings and flew to the boy's country. They landed some distance from the King's palace, where they found feasting still going on, in celebration of the Queen's safe return. For a long time the boy watched and waited and then fell asleep. While he slept the Prince opened the two vases and instantly a beautiful palace formed in front of and facing that of the King. When he woke up, the boy was surprised to find such an exquisite palace and, unsure whether he was dreaming or whether everything was real, he asked the Prince how it had happened. The Prince told him that it had arisen out of the two vases. The boy thanked him and then bade farewell to the Prince, who flew back to his own kingdom.

When the new palace appeared, feasting stopped at the King's palace and everyone looked in awe at the new palace. They wondered who the new King could be, more powerful and wealthy than their own and with such audacity, as to build another palace right in front of their own King's. The King was furious and dispatched two ministers to summon the owner of the new palace. They were astonished to find that the owner of the new palace was none other than the son of the ousted minister, who had gone to rescue the queen, but never returned. They bound him and brought him before the King and the

Queen, who recognised him at once, as did the hundred men who had gone with him to rescue her. Now it was too late for them to do anything but accept the King's punishment for deceiving him.

"Well," said the boy, "I have a long, long story to tell, if your majesty will lend me your ears." He told the King of how he had rescued the Queen and how the hundred men had left him in the cave. He also told him that he had rescued the Prince of the Dragon World, and had been to his kingdom and that it was the Dragon World who had rewarded him with the beautiful palace.

The Queen confirmed that he was really the one who had rescued her from the wizard and that she had been threatened by the hundred men to say that they had rescued her. The King was very angry and ordered the hundred men to be arrested, whipped a hundred times each and imprisoned for life.

Receiving half the kingdom as a reward, the boy became king of his own realm and appointed his father as a minister, while his mother had no work to do. They all lived happily ever after, for what she had told him earlier had come true.

Prosperous and grand:
Wealth of the Gods,
Dusters of brocade,
And sandalwood for fuel.

The Witch Karma Norzom

The beautiful place of Liu dzong had a good governor, who was called Yuchang Gyalpo, but he had a very bad wife. Everybody added the words 'the witch' to her name, so she was always called The Witch Karma Norzom. They had a maid by the name of Balai Kushok, who was no better than the witch. She assisted and provoked the witch to do ugly deeds. So that is the way it was: a good governor with a bad wife and a bad maid.

In addition to being the Governor he was a great businessman and travelled a lot. On one such journey he stayed at a certain house where a widow and her beautiful daughter lived. The daughter was called Shelkar Gyatso and she was so beautiful that the Governor was very attracted to her. Though she was still very young he asked the mother if he could take her as his wife.

"You must have a wife at home. I won't give you my daughter for she is not only very young, she is my only company," answered the mother.

"I have no wife at home," replied the Governor, "and should the girl say she is feeling cold I will clothe her in the best brocade, should she say she is feeling hungry, I will offer her the best food. If she feels thirsty, I will quench her thirst with nectar and will soothe her sorrows in the evergreen gardens."

And it was neither quickly nor willingly that the mother parted with her daughter. He kept on asking and she kept on refusing. After a long time the mother agreed to part with her daughter, her only companion. He dressed her in lovely new clothes and took her to his home on the best steed that he could find.

When they were only a hill's distance from his home, his wife and the maid came to receive him. When she saw them, the girl said, "You have a wife at home. Please grant me leave, I shall not go with you."

"I have no wife and there is no need for you to be fearful or suspicious. But if you are really afraid of those two women you can act as my secretary," said the Governor, and disguised her in men's clothes.

But when his wife saw him with another person, she said, "When you left this place, you were only one man with one horse. Now you return with one more person and a horse. I hope this is not a sign of anything bad, but of an increase in our business." Suspicious, she did not offer him a welcoming drink and walked away.

"Please don't be angry or suspicious, my dear wife," he called after her. "This is only my secretary. Our business is flourishing and I hired him to help me with it."

The witch was placated by his answer, offered him the welcoming drink and together they went home. All the way home she continually glanced at the secretary. She instructed the maid to keep her eyes on "him" too, but they did not notice anything.

When they reached home, the Governor offered the girl a room called 'Happiness-filled Tara Abode', while he and his wife slept in their usual 'Happiness-filled Turquoise Room'. He spent most of his time with the girl, so his wife became very angry and suspicious and sent the maid to spy on them. It did not take long for the sharp-eyed maid to discover the truth. She told the witch that the secretary was not a man but a young and beautiful girl. Hearing this, the witch blazed with anger. With her fangs fully bared and hair flying in all directions, she went to the store-rooms and threw wheat, tea, butter and everything else into the sea, telling the Governor:

"Listen to me once, oh my Lord,
The store-rooms of wheat, tea and butter
Are all but empty.
To Dartse-do you should proceed to buy more."

The Governor made preparations to go. In case the girl felt hungry during his absence, he left her with all manner of delicious foods and nectar to drink when she felt thirsty. He instructed his wife and the maid not to visit the girl's room at all. Excited that the Governor was leaving the very next day and that finally she would be left alone with the girl, she promised to do as he said.

On the very day of the Governor's departure, the witch went to the girl's room with an axe in her right hand, a knife in her left and a sickle at her waist. She called:

"Hear me once, you Shelkar Gyatso:
Open the door, if you will or else,
I will slit your upper parts with my axe,
Your lower parts with my knife,
And your middle part with my sickle,
And leave you unable to get up forever."

Shelkar Gyatso begged:
"Listen to me once, my honourable lady:
Pardon me, please my honourable lady.
All that I have I will hand over to you,
My coral *patuk* I will give you."

Again the witch asked the girl to open the door, but she refused and prostrating towards the witch she pleaded for mercy:

"Oh my honourable lady,
Pardon me, please, I plead unto you.
Everything I own, I shall give to you,
I seek your mercy to spare my life."

The witch became even more furious and while the girl was pleading for mercy from inside, she smashed the door and hit the girl too. Although she was almost dead, the witch did not spare her, but dragged her out and forced her to work. First she was asked to fetch water in a big pail, which she did. Then she was told to roast a hundred bags of wheat, but the girl was unable to do it within the fixed time, so the witch beat her and dragged her into the fire. She was covered with blisters and was as good as dead, when the witch slung her knife, axe and the sickle at her waist, parted her hair on the left and right and dragging the girl out, threw her into the soul-retaining* lake. Having got rid of the girl, she felt contented and relieved. She rewarded the maid for her part in getting rid of the girl and dressing herself in her best clothes, waited for the Governor to return.

Meanwhile, the Governor had made a hasty business trip and returned after only four days. He was so anxious to see his new wife that as soon as he got home, he went straight to the 'Happiness-filled Tara Abode'. He found blood all over the courtyard and asked the witch why there was so much blood.

"The blood is from a ferocious fight between a hen and a monkey, in which the hen was killed," she replied.

---

* Tibetans believe that witches and other super-human beings have their powers and souls retained by other things and not within themselves. It is like Samson, who had his power in his hair.

Then, when he found blood on the steps to the 'Happiness-filled Tara Abode' he asked her why there was blood there also.

"This is because Shelkar Gyatso and I had a duel and she died at my hands."

The Governor almost fainted on hearing that the witch had killed his beautiful, new wife. He rang the big community bell that was used only to summon the public for important meetings. When all the villagers had gathered, he ordered some to go deep into the valley to cut the witch's soul-retaining tree and ordered some to drain the witch's soul-retaining lake. The witch died when her soul-retaining tree was felled and the soul-retaining lake was dried up. Then, he gently lifted the girl's body from the bottom of the lake and tried to cremate it with one load of cypress wood from the right side of the hill, juniper from the left and rhododendron from the front of the hill, but the body would not burn.

"What are you attached to, my young lady, that you will not burn?" he sang.

He thought that she might be attached to his shoes and burnt them without taking them off his feet. Although he burnt his feet, her body still refused to burn. Then he thought that she might be attached to his *chupa* and threw that also into the fire. When the body still would not burn, he said, "You must be attached to me" and jumped into the fire. Then her body burnt and he also died with the girl. At the site of the cremation arose a huge mound of ash.

Along came a man, plodding ahead of his overloaded and miserable donkey. "Oh, here is the mound of ash where our kind and generous governor Yuchang Gyalpo and the girl Shelkar Gyatso were cremated," he said and threw a handful of his donkey's food at the heap of ash. A golden bird flew up out of the heap. He was amazed and threw another handful, up flew a turquoise-coloured bird and joining the golden bird they flew together high into the sky. When nothing happened the third time he threw his donkey's food at the heap of ash, he went on his way and forgot about the two birds.

Everyday the two birds alighted on the roof of the palace of the adjoining kingdom and ate whatever the kind king gave them. The king had no offspring and loved the two birds as if they were his own children. He wondered why they should have such unusual colours and why they always came together at the same time. His curiosity increased day by day, and when he could bear it no more he went to a *lama* and sought his divination. The *lama* told him that it was of auspicious significance and that he should catch them on the 15th day of the fourth month.

When the two birds came as usual for their daily visit and food, the king caught them and took them to the *lama* for further instructions. The *lama* told him to wrap them in expensive cloth and to put the golden bird in a golden box and the turquoise bird in a turquoise box. Then, just as the full moon appeared he should open the two boxes without any delay. The king's curiosity was further increased when the *lama* failed to tell him what would come out of the boxes and what would happen to the birds.

The king counted the days and each day he would sit by the boxes for a long time, watching them and listening to see if he could hear any special sound. At times he almost opened them, but refrained when he remembered that the *lama* had told him not to open them before the full moon.

As the full moon rose, he quickly opened the golden box, out of which appeared a handsome prince — a prince like no other. But he was slow in opening the turquoise box and the princess who appeared from it had a slightly slanted eye, but she was also matchlessly beautiful — like a daughter of the God's realm.

The king and the kingdom, who had been without heirs, now had the most charming prince and princess they had ever seen. They were so happy that they spent the rest of their lives merry-making.

The Witch Mother

In the far corner of a village lived a lonely family, a mother and five sons. The father had died when the children were still very young, leaving their mother to bring them up alone. Through many difficult years she worked hard day and night to support the children. Now that they were all old enough, she thought it high time she got them married and let them lead their own lives. But she did not have enough money to marry them separately, so she married all of them to one beautiful girl. The girl was so pretty that people thought she might be a princess or a heaven-sent goddess to reward the mother for her hard labour and honesty. Her look was the very image of a princess or goddess, but her skills were those of an ordinary, experienced housewife. She helped her mother-in-law in all the day-to-day housework and the older woman was very pleased with her daughter-in-law. The five brothers were also happy and proud of their beautiful and hardworking wife.

The pleasantness and happiness did not last long, as four of the brothers died one after another within four months, until only the youngest was left. After this, the opinion of the people towards the girl changed. She, whom they had once thought to be a princess or a goddess, they now took to be a witch in disguise. The poor boy was in a helpless state. His mother showed no surprise at the deaths of his brothers, neither was his wife any help in finding the cause of their deaths.

One day a friend told him that the girl was a witch and she should be killed or thrown out of the house before he also died. He did not think twice but went home, accused her of being a witch, and told her to leave the house. She became both sad and angry, because he would not listen to any of her pleas or explanations. That very evening she took him to a certain place and made him climb the nearest tree. She tied him to the tree with a big vajra knot and nine ordinary knots and told him to stay there quietly until midnight, when he would witness everything with his own eyes.

At midnight many women gathered under the tree. Some of them were from his own village and some from other villages. He had never seen such a gathering of women either by day or by night. He was trembling with fear as the women came, each more terrible than the last, their hair flying higgeldy-piggeldy in all directions and their eyeteeth protruding from their mouths. Then, in shock, he almost fainted when he saw his own mother come last into the gathering, with much dignity and authority. She was the head of the congregation and seated herself facing the others; it was her turn to bring the nightly sacrifice to the gathering.

When all the women had settled down, his mother brought out a dry human skin and banged it once on the ground. One of the knots binding him came undone. By the time she had banged the skin nine times all the nine ordinary knots had snapped open and only the vajra knot held him to his life. Generally, the witches banged only nine times and, no matter where or how far the victim was hiding, he always appeared, at their disposal, on the ninth bang. But this time, since nothing happened, his mother apologised to the gathering saying that her son had surely been warned. She then chose another person at random and after eating him at their feast, the gathering dispersed for the night.

Still trembling with fright, he climbed down the tree, went home and apologised to his wife, for he was finally convinced that it was not his wife who had killed his brothers.

"I am glad," she said, "that you have seen everything with your own eyes and are convinced that I am not a witch. Now, it is not safe for you to stay like this; you must either run away or kill your mother. If you want to kill her, here is my advice: your mother's life-force enters the red cow that she milks every day. Tomorrow, when she asks you to help her hold the calf, you should stab the mother cow with a knife and kill her. That is the only way you can kill your mother."

The next morning he hid a knife under his *chupa* and asked his mother if he could help her hold the calf.

"Yes, my son, come and help your old mother," she replied.

As his mother milked the cow he noticed the cow's eyes become red and its whole form seemed to change when the mother's life-force re-entered the cow. In a moment of fear and panic, he swung the knife blindly at the cow's head and killed it, instantly his mother also collapsed and died.

He then fed the cow to the vultures and built a stupa over his mother's body, but he did not have the silver paint to complete the stupa. He went to a meditator who lived far into the woods and lamenting his woes, asked for his advice.

"Bring to me whatever you are given by the first person you meet today," said the meditator and sent him away.

On the road he met a girl, who asked him where he was going. He said, "My mother died and I need silver paint for the stupa that I built over her body. So, I am going to look for silver paint."

"I'll give you silver paint," said the girl, and gave him some urine.

"This is strange," he thought, "I asked for silver paint and not urine, and how can I take a woman's urine to the meditator?"

Though he felt awkward and unwilling to take it, he was compelled to obey the meditator's orders. He carried it reluctantly and by the time he reached the meditator's cave there was only a little urine left. The meditator took what was left and applied it to the stupa, which suddenly had a beautiful coating of silver. The young man was speechless.

"Did you recognise the girl who gave you the urine?" asked the meditator.

"No, I didn't."

"That was your own wife in disguise to help you."

When he decided to go in search of her, the meditator stopped him saying, "Now it is impossible to find her. There in no *Karma* for you to live with her any more and she has gone beyond recall. She came from the land of the gods to put a stop to your mother's misdeeds; now that your witch-mother has been removed, she has gone back to her own realm forever."

The Boy who Laughed in his Sleep

The son of Gyal-apchi laughed in his sleep. For some time his mother did not say anything, but when he continued to do it every night, she could not resist asking him why.

"Why do you always laugh so much in your sleep?" she asked.

"It's nothing," he replied, "I laugh for nothing."

"Now, now, there is no need to be shy or afraid of me, I am your mother and you should tell me everything you have on your mind."

"If I must tell you everything, here's the reason: I have a very funny dream of sleeping with half of the sky as my blanket and the other half as my mattress."

When she consulted an astrologer to discover the meaning of the dream, the mother was told, "Your son is destined to become the Emperor of China."

Although she did not really believe the prediction and neither did her neighbours, the news continued to spread all over the country. Very soon, even the Chinese Emperor heard it, but he paid no attention to it. He said, "How can a poor peasant boy become Emperor? I am a very powerful monarch and I shall rule until death terminates my reign." His ministers also agreed with him.

As the days went by the rumour spread further and the Emperor's confidence weakened, so that each night he worried over it. The more he thought about it, the more it tormented him, and he passed many sleepless nights. Finally one day he summoned his ministers and asked them what he should do about this disturbing news. Some told him that there was no reason for concern, while others were of the opinion that something should be done. So, they decided to consult the state astrologer, but he had no better news to tell. He told the Emperor that the boy was definitely destined to rule in his place, no matter what he tried to do to him.

The Emperor thought that killing the boy would be the only solution to give him peace and allow him to remain on the throne. He called the boy to his palace and said, "You are destined to become the ruler of this great Chinese empire and you shall be given the crown if you can bring me a *ha'i-sing-pal* flower, the heart of a *demong* and a daughter of the Northern World."

The boy had no idea where to find these things, but anyway he set out in search of them. He journeyed for many days without knowing in which direction to go, or where to look. After travelling for many more days he ran out of money and, since he did not know where to look, he decided to give up the search. Just at that moment he saw a man with long, deep ears approaching him.

"What a peculiar man you are!" he exclaimed. "Where are you going?"

"I am going nowhere in particular but with these long, deep ears I can hear everything that is being said in all the corners of the world. But the son of Gyal-apchi is luckier than I, for he has the *karma* to become the Emperor of all China."

"I am the son of Gyal-apchi," he said, "and I am going in search of the three things the Chinese Emperor has asked me to bring before I can become the Emperor in his place."

"Oh, how wonderful! Let me help you," he said and they became friends.

While they were travelling from one place to another, they were joined by a man who could stretch his arms over a great distance and a man with an enormous mouth, who called himself the sun-and-moon-eater.

The three men agreed to help the boy to get the things the Emperor had asked for. The man with long arms stretched them over hills, valleys and mountains and brought the *ha'i-sing-pal* flower from the bottom of the Great Sea. Then he brought the heart of a *demong*.

Next the sun-and-moon-eater said to his long-armed friend, "I will eat the sun to make the world dark, then you stretch out your arms and steal the daughter of the Northern World."

Having found the three things he needed, the boy presented them to the Emperor, who could not believe that a small, peasant boy could have obtained what an ordinary human could not. He feared that the boy might be more than an ordinary human being.

Still, the Emperor was unwilling to give the boy the throne. Once again he summoned his ministers and asked them what he should do. Now, that the boy had brought the things he had asked for, it seemed to him that the boy was not merely an ordinary peasant, but the reincarnation of some *Bodhisattva*. The ministers had no other suggestions to offer, than to advise him to kill the boy outright with poison. The Emperor was pleased with their suggestion and planned to host a great feast, to which the boy would be invited as the special guest.

The long-eared friend heard everything the Emperor and the ministers conspired to do and told the boy, "I have heard that the Emperor and his ministers have entered into a conspiracy to poison you. Our long-armed friend will exchange your plate with the Emperor's while our sun-and-moon-eater holds the sun in his mouth. Until then you should not eat." Remembering these instructions carefully, the boy attended the feast.

So, while the sun-and-moon-eater held the sun in his mouth, the long-armed friend stretched out his arms and exchanged the boy's plate with that of the Emperor. When it became dark all of a sudden the Emperor and his ministers were shocked, because no such eclipse was recorded in the almanac. The astrologer himself was in a state of confusion and horror that no eclipse had been revealed by his calculations. They all knew that it was a very bad omen, but did not know what it portended. Their only guess was that the time might have come for the Emperor to abdicate the throne.

The feast continued when the sun reappeared, and all eyes were on the boy waiting for him to die. He ate and drank heartily, but showed no sign of dying. The ministers were surprised and ashamed that they had failed again and, in their eagerness to watch the boy, they did not notice the Emperor die quietly, halfway through the feast. With anger and shame on their faces they got up to leave, but the Emperor did not stir; only then did they realise that he had died instead of the boy.

The boy than became Ruler of the Great Chinese Empire. He kept the daughter of the Northern World as his wife and appointed the three friends as his ministers, and together they ruled wisely for many years.

Prosperity came showering:
Ruler of eighteen huge lands
And nineteen small lands.

The Witch and her Son

There was a place called Aka-kyi and there lived a woman by the name of Goma-kyi. She had a son called Guru Chowang. The woman was a witch—not an ordinary witch, but a ferocious and evil one. She was totally blind to the *Dharma* and could never rouse herself to utter a single word of prayer.

Queer it is that such a fiendish woman should have an incarnate son. He had earned enough merit in his past lives to be born a *Bodhisattva* in this life and was born to this woman to show her the path of religion. So here he was, born to this witch to lead her onto the path of *Buddhadharma*.

He tried every method he could think of to teach her the *Buddhadharma*, or at least to utter a few words of prayer and lift her out of her total ignorance. He told her to recite the six syllable *mantra* every time a bell rang. For this reason he tied bells onto her bag of woollen yarn, on the doorstep, to the top of the door and onto her blankets. This way he thought she could not possibly forget his advice—he would make her remember to say the *mantra*.

But the witch was a witch. She could be nothing better. She was not interested in saying *mantras* and every time a bell rang she had a queasy, uncomfortable feeling. She stuffed ash and cloth into the bells on the door so they would not chime, but she could do nothing about the bells on the yarn bag or the blankets. So, every time these bells rang she said:

"Om mani padme hum, the venom of son Guru Chowang."

This is the way she said the *mantra*. Whenever the bells rang she added dreadful words to it. She took the *mantra* not as an instrument to earn merit, but as a burden, the uttering of which was a waste of time and energy.

Not long afterwards the witch Goma-kyi died. Guru Chowang was neither sad, nor happy at her death. He was not happy because no matter how bad she was, she was his own mother, whom he had been unable to raise from her ignorance. And, he was not sad because he knew that the longer she lived, the more demerits she would accumulate. He went to an astrologer to find out where she would be reborn and was told that she would be reborn a scorpion under the hearth of the fireplace of the local monastery.

He was very eager to find her, to be near her and liberate her from under the hearth. But when he sought the permission of the chief abbot, he was not allowed to dismantle the fireplace. The only way to be near her, even though he could not see her, was to work in the monastery. So he worked as the water-carrier of the monastery. For nine long years he lived near his mother and worked very hard, but he could not do anything to see her or liberate her. When his efforts bore no fruit, even after nine years, he lost hope and sought leave from his work, but was denied. He was told that he would be paid for his services and was requested to stay on. There he found a means to bargain. Instead of accepting money for his work he begged the abbot to allow him to dismantle the fireplace to enable him to find his sinful mother and he promised to build a new one in its place. His request was granted.

The fireplace was so big that it took him three years to dismantle it. Alas, during the three years the scorpion had died and all his labour was in vain, and it took him another three years to rebuild it.

Then he went to the astrologer again, to find out about his mother's next life. He was told that she had taken rebirth as the donkey of a rich merchant in Lhasa. So he ran away from the monastery and went to Lhasa and asked the merchant to hire him as his donkey-boy. He said he would ask for no payment but food and shelter. The merchant was not only able to hire a cheap hand, but he found the boy cheerful and honest too.

While in the service of the merchant, he treated the donkey with compassion and prayed for the swift fulfillment of its present life and a better rebirth. After three years the donkey died and was soon reborn as a human being.

Bodhisattva Guru Chowang's mission was completed and he met his mother once again in the human realm.

The Thief who could Steal a Human

An ageing, poor man and his toothless wife had three grown-up sons. Being very poor their parents had been unable to educate them. They could not read or write, nor did they know any kind of trade. They were completely illiterate and good-for-nothing. As much as their parents wanted to educate and teach them some trade, their poverty lay in their path. So they were walking flesh and bones.

However, they had a rich and kind aunt who lived not very far from their hut. One day their parents took them to this aunt and left them in her custody, for her to do with them as she wished. The aunt was kind and had always wanted to do something for the boys. Whenever she went to see them she asked the parents if she could be of any help to them. They quickly rejected any assistance from her, feeling that she would take away their sons and use them for her own good, but today, now that the boys were at her disposal she felt happy. She fed them good food and gave them nice clothes to wear. For the first time in their lives they saw and tasted a good meal and wore nice clothes. But not many days later the aunt changed her opinion of them and felt them to be no more than extra stomachs to fill. They could not learn anything that she tried to teach them. They grabbed each other's food and tore their clothes while fighting over food and clothes. So she decided to send them away to make them do something on their own. She called them and said, "Some people are skilled in tailoring, some in painting, and some in carpentry. It will be good if each of you learn some kind of trade. I will give you enough money to do so, and if you become very proficient in something, I will even reward you."

The three brothers agreed, so she gave each of them a hundred *sang* and they left to learn a trade. On the way they met three men who asked them where they were going.

"We are three brothers going to learn some trade," they replied.

"We are carpenters," said the three men and agreed to teach the trade to one of the brothers. The eldest brother went with them.

The other two brothers continued on their journey, and again they met three men who also asked them where they were going.

"We are brothers going off to far away lands to learn some trade," they replied.

"We are artists by trade and we will teach it to one of you," said the three men, and the middle brother went with them.

Left alone in a deserted place the youngest brother did not know which way to go. He walked in any direction his feet took him and all the time he was hoping that he would also meet three men to teach him something. For days he walked and walked without meeting anyone. The money his aunt had given him was almost finished and he was afraid that he would never learn anything. He thought it better to die unheard of than to return home without having learnt a trade.

But no, his luck hadn't all run out. One day he met seven men and they asked him where he was going all alone.

"We were three brothers sent by out aunt to learn some trade," he said. "My eldest brother went with three carpenters to learn carpentry and the other went with three artists to learn their trade. Now I am going on alone to learn something."

The seven men did not say what their trade was, but they said that they would teach it to him and took him along with them. He was so happy to meet these seven willing men that he forgot to ask them what their trade was. They were seven expert and well-known robbers, who before robbing anybody forewarned the victim-to-be, even giving the time of their arrival.

On reaching a village they would notify all the rich families that they were coming to rob. Everybody would take double precautions to prevent any theft, but the seven brothers were expert in their trade and the next day everybody would be complaining of some kind of loss: "I lost this and he lost that." The King heard of this and issued a written proclamation: "I challenge you seven brothers to fix a time and steal away my golden vase. If you succeed I shall give you anything you ask for."

"We accept your challenge. We will steal the vase on the fourth day from today and therefore we caution you to take every measure to guard it from our hands," they wrote back to the King.

The King immediately summoned all his ministers and guards and ordered them to observe maximum security, to guard the golden vase and to kill the seven brothers. All around the outer fence of the palace were stationed soldiers, the three-fold gates to the palace were double-locked and a ferocious dog was posted to guard each gate. The vase was kept on a table in the courtyard, surrounded by ministers who protected it day and night. With all these guards and precautions, they were content and satisfied that no thief, however skilled, could come anywhere near the vase let alone steal it.

One day before the given date, one of the brothers was sent to the palace in disguise to study the King's preparations. When they had learnt where the vase was kept and what other precautions were being taken, they made a long tube of bamboo. Then they killed a goat and fixed its bladder to one end of the tube so that it could be blown into a balloon from the other end. That very night three of them took the device and climbed onto the roof of the palace and waited for the ministers to go to sleep. After a long wait, when none of the ministers would go to sleep, they threw lots of dust in the air. Soon every minister was rubbing his eyes and not paying any attention to the vase. In the meantime, they quickly extended the long bamboo tube and put the bladder into the vase. When they blew through the tube into the bladder, it inflated and filled the vase so they were able to lift it away and escape with it.

When the dust had settled and the ministers had cleaned their eyes, they found the vase missing. They cursed and scolded the outer guards for letting the thieves in, while the guards cursed the ministers for not keeping a good watch. They were all cursing each other and there was a babble of words flying in every direction; everywhere was chaos.

The King was the least surprised when he learnt that the seven brothers had stolen the vase. He did not blame or scold anyone, but sent a messenger asking them to return it, repeating his promise to pay for it and give them whatever they desired. He also allowed them to practise their trade without fear of punishment from him. After receiving a handsome payment for the vase, the seven brothers left the town to pursue their trade in another region.

For eight long years the boy who had gone to learn a decent trade, learned the trade of thieves from these seven brothers. Sometimes he assisted them, while at other times he went alone to steal. After eight years he had become very proficient in his trade and he decided to return home unsure whether his aunt would approve of his skill or not.

At home the other two brothers had returned. One had become a very good carpenter and the other an artist. Their parents and aunt were very happy, they offered butter-lamps to the gods as thanksgiving and prayed for further prosperity. The two brothers worked so hard that within a year they had moved their parents from the tiny hut into a decent house. Wealth flowed in and prosperity waited on their doorstep. Their parents, once looked down upon by the other villagers were now an object of envy. The aunt rewarded the boys for their hard work and so began a happy future.

Then the youngest boy came home. His parents, aunt and two brothers thought that he must have learned a very special trade that it had taken him so much time, and were very eager to know what he had learnt. They celebrated his return and feasted for many days. But whenever he was asked of his trade, he always replied: "I have learnt a very profitable craft," and would answer nothing more. When they persisted in their questions he finally told them that he had learnt the art of robbery. They were very angry and disappointed and told him to leave the house, because he was unfit to live in their simple but honest family; where he went was up to him.

Just as he was about to leave, his aunt called and consoled him, saying that even robbing is an art. "I will test you in your trade and see if you have learnt it well," she said, "and if you can steal what I say, I shall reward you too, just as I rewarded your brothers."

Hearing these words from his once strict aunt was more than an ordinary consolation. He agreed to undergo the test, being confident of his skill, and knowing that there was nothing in this world that he could not steal.

The aunt said, "You are to steal my brocade quilt, but if you fail in this you must practice your trade no more." She thought a quilt was something nobody could steal, as it would be in complete contact with her body, and was surprised when he agreed to her challenge.

Early in the morning on the day he was to steal the quilt he went fishing. He caught a lot of fish and gave them to his aunt, who he knew was very fond of fish. She thanked him, ate some and left the rest in her kitchen. While she was busy with the fish, he studied the rooms for possible ways to get in and noticed that she had forgotten to block the chimney.

That night, while his aunt was fast asleep, he climbed onto her roof and miaowed like a cat down the chimney. She woke up and thought that a cat was eating her fish. While she went to the kitchen to chase it away, he climbed down to her bedroom and stole the quilt leaving an imitation in its place. When she found no cat in the kitchen and that her fish was safe, the aunt came back and went soundly to sleep again.

In the morning, when she found her own quilt missing, she cried out in astonishment. She begged him to return the quilt, offering to pay any price for it.

"Oh, my loving aunt, this is nothing," he boasted playfully, "I could even steal you!"

The aunt appreciated that he was very skilled in his trade, but this boast to steal a human being was something unimaginable. "If you can steal me I will give you half of my property," she said, "But if you fail, I shall kill you." She threatened him thinking it would stop him stealing and boasting. She also warned him that he must really steal her away, that getting her out of the house by force would not suffice. He agreed to her terms and told her that he would come to steal her on the third day.

"This is impossible," she said to herself, "How can a human being be stolen?"

He lost no time in making preparations and went to his brothers to ask for their help. He asked the carpenter to make a wooden man like himself and asked the artist to paint it. When finished it was just like him. He did not tell them what he wanted it for, but thanked them profusely and busied himself with other things. First he killed a sheep, then filled its bladder with blood which he tied around the neck of the wooden man.

On the third day, as soon as it was dark he started digging an underground passage into his aunt's house. Before dawn he reached the house and looked around. As he kept poking his head out of the hole his aunt woke up. Slowly she picked up a sword and as she swung at him, he held up the wooden man and the blood from the bladder spilt out.

"There goes my poor and not-too-clever nephew," she thought. She was thrilled and laughed so much that she could not stop for a long time—swaying here and there, back and forth like a drunkard—so she did not feel herself carried away. He pulled her slowly into the hole and took her to his house, where he woke her out of her trance. He said, "I have stolen you from your own house without compulsion; now may I have the reward, please?" Like the other people of the village she was astonished by his dexterity. In shame, without saying a word, she rewarded him with half her property.

Then there was a feast. He invited his parents, brothers and other relatives and they feasted to their heart's content. He then promised not to practise his trade any more, and they all lived happily ever after.

Nun Gyurme Saldon's Son

Of the hundreds of nunneries spread throughout Tibet, there was one called Migyur-Ling with a few hundred nuns of different ages and levels of spiritual development. The abbess was a woman of very stern countenance and of high principles. She would tolerate no men to enter the nunnery even if they were monks. She even forbade them from coming within the boundaries of the estate. Any meeting or business matters had to be brief and take place in her presence.

Nun Gyurme Saldon was a lonely nun because nobody came to visit her. She was obedient and devoted all of her time to reading the scriptures and praying and was seldom seen outside her room. Then a strange thing happened, she gave birth to a charming little boy, who was named Ling-tuk Ser-gyi Gya-Ling. The news of this strange incident spread far and wide, and the helpless Gyurme Saldon was thrown out of the nunnery and sent to live in a small hut just below. The news of the birth of a son to a nun did not travel only to human ears, a lone wizard in the forest also heard it. He had always yearned for company and felt that the nun would be only too happy to let him adopt her son.

Somehow, the boy knew that the wizard was coming and told his mother, "I have a feeling that somebody will come to our house and take me away." He told her to hide him carefully, close all the doors and windows and let the dog loose.

"Who would come to see such poor people as us?" asked his mother. "Nobody has and nobody ever will come to our house."

"No, no, mother," he told her. "Somebody will definitely come to our house." He begged her to do as he had asked.

Finally, she hid him in a big pot, closed and bolted the doors and windows, tied the dog up outside, and waited for the unknown guest to arrive.

In the distance there appeared a black man on a black horse with a black bow in his hand, followed by a ferocious, black dog coming in the direction of their house. Soon the wizard was at the door. He knocked and called out,

"Listen to me once, Nun Gyurme Saldon of Migyur-Ling nunnery:
Give me a place to stay for the night,
And show me the direction of tomorrow's journey."

Gyurme Saldon responded:

"If you are an up-tavelling man
Please travel upwards.
And if you are travelling down
Please continue downwards.
I have no place for you to stay,
And no direction to point you on your way."

Once again the wizard asked the nun to allow him to stay for the night and show him the way, but the nun would not open the door even a crack, fearing that the wizard would take away her son, her only companion. The wizard then lost his temper and broke down the door. He looked all over the tiny house, turned everything upside-down but did not find the boy. He became even more furious when the nun denied having a son at all. He beat her and left her almost dead.

The boy then came out of hiding, and though the wizard had long since gone, he was still sweating and trembling with fear. He clung to his mother and said, "Mother, instead of being any help to you in earning our bread, I'm only a nuisance and danger to your life. I'll go and try to work for the King."

"You need not go," said his mother. "We'll be all right with what I earn and eating *doma*." But the boy left anyway.

The King was surprised to see a small boy asking for employment. He told him that he had no need of an extra servant, but the boy begged the King to take him and promised to work as hard as his tiny frame would allow. Reluctantly, the King hired him and, as a test, he was first asked to look after the hundred horses. Though the boy had never looked after horses, nor even ridden any, he was a gifted horseman. He took them to places where there was plenty of grass and water. He was very fond of them and they in turn obeyed him and neighed his praises every morning when he came to take them grazing. After a short time, the hundred horses had multiplied into a herd of a thousand thoroughbreds.

The King was astonished at the boy's ability and the ten-fold increase in the number of his horses. He wanted to find out whether it was merely a coincidence or a result of the boy's efforts. So next he appointed him to look after his sheep and when they also multiplied ten-fold, he asked him to look after the yaks and then the pigs. Not only did these animals increase in numbers, other strange things happened; once barren lands turned into beautiful green pastures, rivers flowed in dry valleys and trees grew in deserted places. The kingdom was blessed with a prosperity it had never known before.

The King had a daughter named Shang-shang Go-yog, who was fair and lovely. Kings of many countries had set their hearts on taking her as their wife, but she only loved the boy. Like any other shepherd, while following his herd he would exchange gossip with the other shepherds. He heard many stories and learnt what the talk of the town was. During one such conversation he heard that the kings of Benda, the Hor Kingdom; Gorkha, the Turquoise Kingdom; Shang-shung, the Wealth-filled Kingdom and Belyul, the Scarf Kingdom, were arriving to contest for the girl's hand in marriage. So one day he called the girl and said, "Shang-shang Go-yog la, the kings of four different kingdoms are coming to seek your hand in marriage. Will you go with them or stay with me to be a shepherdess?"

"I'd rather stay with you."

"But what will you do if your father won't allow you to stay with me and forces you to marry one of them?"

"I won't marry any of them, but will surely stay with you, my shepherd boy."

Meanwhile the King, pleased by the boy's efficiency and the good fortune and prosperity that he had brought with him, had decided to appoint him as one of his special advisers. He summoned the boy and told him, "From this moment on you will not go out with the animals but will remain here as my special adviser. You will be known as Zhi-la Akhui Dok-dok."

The boy replied, "If you won't allow me to look after the animals I love, I shall resign from your service."

The King was very angry that such a small boy had the audacity to refuse his orders. He wanted to punish the boy severely, but remembered that his kingdom had found prosperity only after the boy had become his servant. Still, the boy had refused to obey him, which nobody had ever done before, he could not let him go without some punishment.

"You shall plough the field behind the palace, which has given no yield for the last nine years," the King ordered. "If you can plough it and get a harvest from it, I shall let you have your way."

Losing no time, he went to work on the hard, barren field. He worked so hard that where other people took twelve days to plough a piece of land he took only one, and very soon the field was green with different crops. When the harvest season came, the yield was of such astonishing quantity and quality that the swollen stores cracked. Never before had the King been concerned by an over-abundance of grain, but he was worried now and ordered new stores to be built. The King was so delighted that he told the boy to do whatever he wanted.

"I want to remain a shepherd," said the boy, "but I would like you daughter Shang-shang Go-yog to bring me my midday meal."

The King was so grateful for his achievements, that he granted his wish willingly.

On the following day Shang-shang Go-yog went out to give him his lunch and called out, "You must be hungry and thirsty. Come and have your meal." She was full of love and affection for him.

"Bring the meal-bag from the left side of the *dzo*," he replied.

She thought it very strange that the meal-bag should be taken from the left side of the *dzo* only. He had never been so strange and irritable like this before. She did not take the meal-bag but asked him to come to her. When he repeated that the meal-bag should be taken from the left side of the *dzo*, she became irritated and was about to leave when he reminded her, "Your father sent you to give me my meal. Why do you want to go away without serving it?" He called her closer to him and begged her not to go away, but to stay with him. He said, "Many kings are coming to plead for your hand, but you shouldn't go with any of them. Please stay with me."

"If it is my father's wish, I will have to marry and nothing will be able to stop it. But, I will ask my father to send you as my servant, so that we will not be parted."

Just as he had foretold, the kings of four different kingdoms came to ask for the girl's hand in marriage. After many days of discussion and consultation with astrologers, it was finally decided to give Shang-shang Go-yog to the king of Belyul, the Scarf Kingdom.

She told her father that she would marry the King only if Zhi-la Akhui Dok-dok was sent with her as her servant. The King did not want to lose Akhui Dok-dok but was left with no choice, and had to send him with her.

And so the three of them, the girl, the King of Belyul and Zhi-la Akhui Dok-dok started their long journey towards the land of Belyul.

"Shall I sing you a song?" asked Akhui Dok-dok.

"Yes," said the King, "but a sweet song, please."

So he sang:

"The King of Belyul, the stone under the bridge,
Lady Shang-shang Go-yog, the plank on the top,

And Akhui Dok-dok, the river under the bridge.
What will the stone do, if the plank is washed away by the river?"

"What a melodious song, can you sing us another?" the King asked.

"Yes, but I'll sing only when we reach the top of the mountain."

On the top of the mountain he sang:

"The King of Belyul, the bamboo stick on the mountain top,
Lady Shang-shang Go-yog, the flag on the bamboo stick,
And Akhui Dok-dok, the northern wind on the mountain top.
What will the bamboo do if the wind blows the flag away?"

The King asked him to sing again, but he said he would sing when they reached the plains.

Just as he had promised he sang this song when they reached the plains and came across a ranch:

"The King of Belyul, the square ranch in the northern wilderness,
Lady Shang-shang Go-yog, the sheep in the ranch,
And Akhui Dok-dok, the wolf from the wilderness.
What will the ranch do if the sheep is eaten by the wolf?"

The King found the three songs very attractive, but could not understand their hidden meaning. He was so tired from travelling that he asked them to stop for a rest. While he was asleep, Shang-shang Go-yog and Akhui Dok-dok ran away, leaving him alone in the wilderness.

Akhui Dok-dok said to Shang-shang Go-yog: "I am going to visit my mother because I haven't seen her for a long time. You can go to your father," and left her to find her own way.

When she reached her father's palace, he scolded her for not going with the King of Belyul.

"You have disgraced me with your behaviour. Now I shall give you to the first man who comes to my door tomorrow."

It so happened that the fool who looked after the King's pigs heard this and went early the next morning to ask for fire. The King gave him not only fire, but also his daughter. The fool was very happy, but she was at a loss. Sad as she was, she tried to make herself happy with him and adjust to their poverty.

Meanwhile, Akhui Dok-dok had gone to his mother. It had been so long since he left home, that she had nests in her hair and piles of dirt in her eyes. Lamenting his absence she had neither washed her face, nor combed her hair since he had gone. At first she could not believe that he was her own son, or that he had been working for the King since he left home. But she was overjoyed to see him alive. After this happy reunion he promised to visit her more often and left to work for the King again.

One day when Shang-shang Go-yog and the fool were in the pig-stye, telling each other stories and picking lice from each other's hair, Akhui Dok-dok threw a stone onto the roof.

"I dont know whether it is auspicious or inauspicious that someone should throw stones at our pig-stye," she said.

Then he threw the ring that she had given him before.

"No, it was not inauspicious, because a ring has also fallen into my lap," she said, knowing that Akhui Dok-dok was nearby.

"If our karma favours us, we will meet even in a pig-stye," he said. They hugged each other tight for joy and ran away leaving the poor fool crying. The fool went to the top of the mountain and cried:

"She is not there, she is not there:

My lady Shang-shang Go-yog is not there."

Poor fool, it is pity that nobody was there to hear his cry and help him.

In the meantime, Akhui Dok-dok took Shang-shang Go-yog to her father's palace, where the two were married. They were given a part of the kingdom as a wedding present. Then Akhui Dok-dok invited his mother to stay with them, and they all lived happily ever after.

The Hoopoe Family

Once there lived a father and mother hoopoe. They had been living together for many years, migrating from one place to another, never deciding where they should settle down. The mother hoopoe was always anxious to settle down in one place, have children and lead a family life, but the father hoopoe was interested only in travel and adventure. He was not a good husband.

After many years of patient waiting, the mother hoopoe finally begged the father hoopoe to let her have a family of her own instead of loving and cuddling other birds' chicks. Without waiting for a reply, she laid some eggs and sat down to hatch them. The father hoopoe had no option, but to settle down and go hunting for food, while the mother hoopoe stayed at home and hatched eggs. So they settled there and father hoopoe went out in search of food for the family.

First, he went to the King's garden and stole a juicy flower but, unfortunately, on the way back, it slipped and fell from his beak. He flew down to pick it up, but there was nothing left; the flower was crushed and useless. All his labour and the risks he had taken were in vain. He was sad that his dear wife would not be able to enjoy such a treat. So, he went to look for something else in a rich man's garden, where he found ample food both to eat and to take home. He ate till his stomach almost burst and from the great choice of food available he stole one ripe pea.

At the bank of a river he hired a scorpion, an ant, a beetle and a stink-bug to help him peel and clean the pea. Then he went to a *chang-ma* and bought a good quantity of *chang* to offer to his hired hands.

He also promised to repay them handsomely. They worked harder and harder as the *chang* had its effect and each insect volunteered to sing a song to start their tiny harvest. Each was eager to sing before the others, until finally it was agreed that the stink-bug would sing first. He sang:

"With this way of walking and the smell,
I feel I'm like a doctor's medicine bag."

Then the ant sang:
With this way of walking and my curvy waist,
I feel I'm like a beautiful lass."

Then the beetlė sang:
"With this way of walking and my special sound,
I feel I'm like a man from *Hor*."

Finally the scorpion sang:
"With this way of walking and these two horns,
I feel I'm like a beautiful *dzo*."

When their work was done, the hoopoe took the pea to the river-side to sift and wash it, but all the pieces of the pea were swept away and he had nothing left to take home. With so much labour spent once more in vain, he was even sadder than when he lost the juicy flower.

Meanwhile, the eggs had hatched into five beautiful chicks and the mother hoopoe and her children waited eagerly for many days for the father hoopoe to return with some food. But he did not return. She and the chicks were hungry, but she could not leave them to go hunting for food or to search for father hoopoe, because they were too small to take care of themselves.

After more waiting, she lost her patience and went in search of father hoopoe. She found him with his four friends and scolded him, "You have been roaming around without thinking of me and the children, we have been starving without food for so many days!" Then she abused him with all the curses she could think of, till she thought he would repent and apologise. But the more she spoke, the more angry he became, yet he said nothing until she had finished, and then used his physical strength to show his anger. He beat her so severely that she died; then he went home and killed all the children. For a while he thought he had accomplished what he wanted, but when he realised that mother hoopoe had not merely fainted, but was really dead, he was sorrowful and shed tears.

Nevertheless, it did not take him long to forget the death of his wife and children and regain his spirits. He looked forward to days of travel and adventure and befriended another scorpion. He thought that the scorpion would be a good companion when he went to steal food and suggested that they should both go to the King's garden, telling tales of the beautiful garden and the plentiful food one could find there. The scorpion was easily tempted and crawled towards the garden, while the hoopoe flew and waited on a tree for the scorpion to arrive. No sooner had the scorpion entered the garden than the gardener saw him, threw a stone and killed him. The hoopoe was very sad at the unfortunate deaths of his children and his wife, and his friend the scorpion, and feeling very lonely he sang this song in memory of his dear wife:

"Sweet mother hoopoe,
Rise up and do not sleep.
To home we shall go,
To eat delicious pea skins."

The Dog Skin King

Many years ago, there lived a mother and her three daughters, Dekyi, Dolkar and Dolma. The family was neither very rich nor very poor, but they were contented with their simple life.

One day a bulky dog approached the mother and asked her to keep a small bag of *tsampa* for him until he returned to fetch it. The girls laughed at their mother for heeding a dog's request and at the dog for what it had just said. But they kept the bag of *tsampa* for the dog all the same.

One year, two years and three long years they kept the bag of *tsampa* and waited for the dog to return to fetch it, but the dog did not come. So they ate the *tsampa* thinking that he would never come and that even if he did, they could simply fill his bag with their own *tsampa*.

The very next day the dog came plodding along and asked for his bag of *tsampa*. They tried desperately to fill the small bag with their own *tsampa* but somehow they just could not fill it. Finally, they had to tell the truth and agreed to listen and comply with anything he wished by way of compensation.

"All right then, give me one of your daughters," said the dog to the mother. The family had no alternative but to comply with his strange wish. The mother packed some *tsampa* and meat for her eldest daughter Dekyi and some bones and crumbs for the dog before sending them on their way together. The dog led the way as they travelled and the girl followed him. She panted and cursed him for the speed at which he went and because she hated the very thought of being the wife of an ugly dog, she hated him too.

They stopped at the bank of a river for a rest and to have their midday meal.

"You eat *tsampa* and meat and give me some bones and crumbs to eat," said the dog.

"Of course, I will eat *tsampa* and meat and give you your crumbs and bones. How can I give meat and *tsampa* to an ugly dog like you?"

After eating lunch the dog said, "Now we have to cross the river. Should I carry you across or will you carry me?"

"Why should I carry you?" replied Dekyi. "You are a dog and I am a human being; you should carry me."

Instead of proceeding further, the dog returned Dekyi to her mother and asked for the second daughter, Dolkar.

The mother then offered her second daughter, Dolkar, who was no more willing than her sister and faring no better with her, the dog also returned her to her mother and asked for the youngest daughter, Dolma.

As before, the mother packed some *tsampa* and meat for her, some bones and crumbs for the dog and bade her youngest daughter farewell.

The dog led the way and the girl followed him dutifully, until they stopped at the riverside for a rest.

"Give me some bones and crumbs," said the dog. "You can eat *tsampa* and meat."

"Oh no," said the girl, "this cannot be. Though you are a dog you are still my husband. We will share the meat and *tsampa*," and gave him a lump of meat.

After the meal the dog said, "We have to cross the river. Should I carry you or will you carry me across?"

"You are small and might get drowned," Dolma replied. "I will carry you across." Putting him on her shoulder, she carried him across.

Finding that the youngest daughter was not only willing to share her food, but also to carry him across the river, the dog felt Dolma had the proper qualities of a wife and decided to keep her.

In the course of their wandering, Dolma had two puppies by the dog. Then one day, they came within sight of a magnificent palace.

Dolma looked at it in awe and imagined herself as its queen, but she decided she must accept the fate of her karma and remain a faithful wife to the dog.

When they were nearer to the palace the dog told Dolma to stay behind, while he went ahead to beg for some food. Despite Dolma's insistence that she wanted to accompany him, he went alone. At the palace gate many dogs attacked and killed him. Dolma felt forlorn and sat there crying bitter tears.

After a while, as she lay lamenting over the death of her husband many horsemen rode up and addressing her as "Your Majesty", asked her to accompany them to the palace. She protested that she was not a queen, but the poor wife of a dog, who had been killed by the dogs at the palace gate. Nevertheless, the horsemen placed her on a horse and took her to the palace.

Within the palace, a handsome, young king sat on a golden throne with a silver throne on his right and a turquoise throne on his left. The king was none other than her own husband, who had been roaming the country disguised as a dog, in search of a suitable bride. She was the one he had chosen after many years of searching. The young

King patted the two puppies and they instantly turned into two royal children. He seated them on the silver throne and offered Dolma the turquoise throne. All the ministers received them with honour and respect. When Dolma's two sisters, Dekyi and Dolkar heard her story, that she now lived in peace and prosperity, they were envious of her and regretted their own lost chances.

The Meditator and the Thief

Once a simple, pious man lived in a cave at the far end of a village. His only notable possession was a set of seven silver bowls for offering water to the gods on his altar. These bowls were very dear to him, not because they were made of silver, but because seven bowls of clean water was the only thing he could offer to the gods.

A thief living in the same village saw the meditator's treasure and was tempted to steal it. He thought the meditator would be easy prey like other meditators who easily fell victim to numerous thieves because of their extreme devotion to religious duties and carelessness over their material belongings. Even if they caught a thief, they did not punish him severely because of the compassion within their hearts.

One night, the thief set out for the meditator's cave and peeping in saw that he was asleep. Slowly, he shoved himself into the cave and extended his hand to steal the bowls. Unfortunately, for him, the meditator was not sleeping, but sitting upright, meditating. The meditator let the hand come right up to the bowls, then caught it and beat it harshly, chanting:

"I take refuge in the Guru,
I take refuge in the Buddha,
I take refuge in the Dharma,
I take refuge in the Sangha." Then he set the thief free.

The beating hurt so much that the thief was almost in tears, but, somehow, he was able to memorise the meditator's words. He recited them to himself as he went home, nursing his bruised hand.

On the way he saw a couple of huge figures like horsemen coming in his direction from the other side of the bridge. They were ghosts, but when they heard his prayers, they disappeared. Though he had been unable to steal anything, he was saved from the terrifying ghosts.

So the saying goes, that merely uttering a prayer can save you from the evils and dangers that lie in your path.

The Scheming Sparrow

A pigeon and a sparrow lived quite close to each other. They were very friendly and lived in the most neighbourly manner. However, that was a very long time ago.

One day the pigeon felt like playing a joke on the sparrow. She went to the sparrow's nest and playfully threw out all the soft lining, piled it in front of the nest, and went in search of the sparrow. On meeting the sparrow, she said, "Friend, a wool merchant has stationed himself in front of your nest." The sparrow returned to her nest and saw the damage that had been done to it, but neither said nor did anything, deciding instead to wait to get her revenge on the pigeon.

A few days later, the sparrow went to the pigeon's nest in her absence, killed all the young birds and went in search of her neighbour.

"Friend, last time there was a wool merchant in front of my nest," said the sparrow. "Now there is a butcher right on your doorstep and he has all the meat you could want in the world."

Immediately, the pigeon suspected something and flew back to her nest. She was very upset to find her young ones dead and went in search of the sparrow.

As soon as they met, they quarrelled and fought fiercely. The pigeon threw thorns at the sparrow's breast and wounded her seriously (the black mark of which can be seen on a sparrow's breast even today.) When the other birds heard about the fight, they could not believe that two usually friendly birds should engage in such a useless squabble. They stopped the fight and took them to court to try them.

The court tried them both and sentenced the sparrow to receive the death penalty, having found her guilty of committing murder, while the pigeon was sent into exile for having started the fight. The sparrow was handed over to a hawk for execution. The hawk grasped the tiny sparrow in his mighty claws and flew up into the sky.

High up in the air the sparrow called out, "Uncle hawk, please loosen your grip a bit, I want to make my last wish."

The hawk loosened his grip, and the sparrow said, "Tell my red-breasted sister Dhili that the days of wearing coral and turquoise are over for me."

Again, sometime later, the sparrow said that she had a second wish to make, and begged the hawk to loosen his grip. The hawk took pity on the sparrow and loosened his grip still more.

"Tell my friend Ata Ga-hu that the days of frequent journeys and exciting adventures are now over for us," said the sparrow.

Again, for the third time, the sparrow begged the hawk to loosen his grip for her to speak her third wish. No sooner had the hawk relaxed his grasp, than the sparrow escaped and hid in a yak's horn. Unable to do anything else, the hawk sat on the horn to wait for the sparrow to come out. He was very scared that the court would execute him if it heard of the sparrow's escape. For two days he sat on the horn waiting patiently, but he was not only tired, he was also very hungry and thirsty.

Meanwhile, the sparrow was getting annoyed with the hawk's patience. She knew that if she made any attempt to leave the horn, she would meet with certain death. At last a very bright idea struck her; pretending to be an old frog she cried,

"I am going to die like my father, who was killed by another hawk."

"How was your father killed?" asked the hawk.

"When my father was being chased by a hawk, he also hid in a *yak's* horn, but it was a very weak hiding place. The hawk dipped himself in the water, rolled in the sand, flew high up into the sky and dived down on the horn, which, with a thundering flap of his wings, he smashed and so killed my poor father. Then he ate him up."

As soon as the hawk heard of this clever stunt, he consoled the frog (sparrow), assuring him that he would not do such a thing and that he was not as wicked as the other hawk. But he flew away quietly, dipped in the water, rolled in the sand, then flew high up into the sky and swooped down onto the horn, but it was he who was smashed into pieces and he died instantly.

The sparrow then emerged from the horn, sat on the hawk's head and laughing, flew away.

The Adventures of the Seven Sheep

Long, long ago, there was a man named Ji-zin-mey who had seven sheep. He was very fond of them—he fed them with lots of nice grass, took them to beautiful pastures, and they gave him abundant milk and wool in return. In all his years as a simple and poor shepherd he never had any other sheep like these seven. And, of all the masters they had had during their lives, none of the seven sheep had had a master like Ji-zin-mey. He was very happy with them and they were also very happy with him.

One day a crow flew inside his tent and was drinking milk from the milk-pail when Ji-zin-mey came in. Because he came in suddenly, the crow panicked and was too frightened to find its way out; it flew wildly inside the tent and striking its stomach against a pole, it died. The man laughed and laughed uncontrollably; he laughed till his guts burst and he died too.

The sheep were very sad and decided that they should take their master's body to Lhasa, and lay it before *Jowo Rinpoche* for blessings, as a final tribute to their kind master. So they journeyed for many days carrying his body in turn. One day they met a wolf, who asked them, "Where are you going without a master, and what is that you are carrying? You all are very fat and it is time for me to eat you up."

"We are taking our deceased master's body to Lhasa," they said and pitifully begged for their lives to be spared. "Please do not eat us now; you can eat us on our return when each of us will have a lamb and there will be even more of us to eat than now."

After much pleading the wolf finally agreed to spare them for the time being, on the condition that they must meet him at the same spot when they returned.

Their hearts not yet free of sorrow over the death of their master, they had encountered the further sorrow of having to die at the hands of a strange wolf, after so many years of peace and prosperity.

In Lhasa they laid the body of their master before *Jowo Rinpoche.* They also made offerings in his name and prayed for the early return of their master to the human realm.

It took them many months, and during that time each of them had a lamb. After completing their task, they returned. When they neared the place where they were to meet the wolf, the older ones wept but the young ones played about joyfully innocent of the fate that awaited them. At this moment a hare came by and asked them why they were so sorrowful. When they told him about the wolf and the fate awaiting them, the hare said, "If this is so, I can help but only if each of you carry me in turn." The sheep accepted his offer and each of them carried him in turn.

On the way they found a *charu* and the hare told them that it would be useful and made one of them carry it. Then they found a piece of cloth which, too, the hare said would have some use and another of them carried that. Lastly, they found a piece of paper, which they also took with them. When they reached the place, where they had agreed to meet the wolf, the hare made them stop and commanded in a loud voice:

"Set the Circular Ear-ring Seat!" The sheep laid out the *charu*.

"Lay down His Excellency's mat!" the hare ordered again, and the sheep laid the piece of cloth on the *charu*.

The hare seated himself on it and commanded: "Now bring His Excellency's Order-paper." The sheep handed him the piece of paper.

Pretending to read from the paper, the hare announced loudly:

"This is the order of the Emperor of the entire Black-Haired-Tibetan Empire, that whosoever attacks these fourteen sheep, who are returning home after doing pious deeds in Lhasa, must bear in mind that he will be beheaded."

The wolf, who was listening from a nearby hideout, heard the frightening decree, and immediately ran for his life.

On the way he met a *mirgö*, who asked him why he was running in such a fright. The wolf told him the whole story.

"Don't be frightened," said the *mirgö*, "it is one of those pranks the hare is used to playing in everybody. Let us go back and fight him face to face."

Even with the *mirgö's* reassuring company, the wolf was not willing to go back and face the hare, who had direct orders from the Emperor to execute anyone attempting to harm the lives of the fourteen sheep. But, finally they tied themselves together and went to meet the hare.

When the hare saw the wolf and the *mirgö* coming together, he asked the wolf, "Is this the fat dri that you said you would bring along in your place?" and hit the *mirgö* on the head with a stick. At once the *mirgö* became suspicious of the wolf's tale and took flight dragging the wolf behind him. By the time he reached his cave, he found that the wolf was dead.

That was the end of the wolf. The sheep thanked the hare and returned to their village in peace. Their lives returned once more to the good old days, except that they were without their loving master.

The Old Couple and their Three Sons

Years and years ago there lived an old couple who had three sons. As time went on they grew up into three fine, healthy, clever, young men, each of whom was given a good share of money to help him lead his own life. All of them put the money to good use and were able to increase it three-fold. They were as happy with their prosperity, as their parents were proud to see their sons doing so well.

One day the parents called them together and asked, "By whose grace and kindness are you happy and prosperous now?"

"By the grace of The Three Jewels, in particular and also through the kindness of our loving parents," replied the two elder sons.

But the youngest son said, "My happiness and prosperity are due to the Three Jewel's grace, but also to my own ability and determination."

The parents were very angry at his tart and ungrateful answer and expelled him from the family. He was very sad and realised that he should not have given such a hurtful reply, though he thought that what he had said was nothing but the truth that he felt in his heart. Knowing that it was too late to apologise or rectify his mistake, he packed his belongings and went to live in the nearby town. Not long after his arrival there his fortunes increased even more, and he married a rat by the name of Zhi-mi. She was like no other rat, she not only did all the housework, but also advised him on business matters and, thereby, his wealth increased. Everything seemed to go right with him after he married the rat, so he was content.

Then, one hot summer day, the parents once again called their three sons together and asked them to bring a piece of ice. The youngest could think of no way of obtaining a piece of ice in such hot weather and thought that this would be a second disappointment for his parents. With his head drooped in a mournful manner and tears rolling down his cheeks, he went home and related the impossible task to his wife.

"Don't worry," said the rat. "I will get a piece of ice for you," She then gave him a piece of ice that she had produced from nowhere.

Without waiting for her instructions or asking her how she got the ice, he ran to his parents' house in great excitement. The two brothers looked in surprise at the ice. They could not believe their eyes when he brought the ice in such a hot day and in such a short time. They were ashamed to ask him how or from where he had gotten it, but his parents were very pleased with him and showered him with plentiful compliments.

Months later, in the middle of winter, when it was so cold that even iron cracked, when the whole landscape had turned bleak and desolate and the trees were naked, the parents once again called the boys and told them to bring beautiful and sweet-smelling flowers. The youngest son was once again heavy-hearted. Just as he could think of no way of getting a piece of ice in summer, he could think of no way of getting any flowers in that bleak mid-winter. "My faithful wife might have produced ice for me in summer, but how can she help me obtain flowers in the dead of winter," he thought.

When he reached home his wife consoled him and promised that she would bring flowers for him. Again, out of nowhere, she produced a bunch of the most beautiful flowers in the world. Holding them delicately in his hands, he presented them to his parents. They at once reprimanded the other two sons for their failure in both tests, and said that it was the youngest son who was really faithful and hard-working.

Years went by, and when the ageing parents realised that death awaited them nearby, they called the three sons for a family reunion feast, to which each of them brought his wife. The two older brothers boasted about their own wives' beauty, and laughed and joked about their younger brother's wife. Their wives also joined them in making ridiculous remarks about the rat. However, the parents said nothing, because it was he who produced ice in summer and flowers in winter and they thought that this might also be some trick.

When it came to the feast, the poor rat could not eat anything, because the eldest brother's wife had trodden on her tail. To add to the pain and humiliation, she was asked to serve the meal and wash the dishes.

Without a murmur of complaint or hesitation, the rat got up to obey their orders. But when she stepped forward to serve, the other wife trod so hard on her tail that the rat skin came off, revealing the most beautiful girl from the Nāgā realm, the kingdom beneath the Earth. All of them looked astounded and stared at each other, speechless. The youngest son was also surprised, but now he understood the reason for his prosperity and good fortune. But the girl, as if ignorant of what had happened, continued to serve the food and wash the dishes, more like an experienced servant than a princess from the Nāgā realm. The wives of the other two brothers were ashamed of themselves.

The Princess then invited her husband and his ageing parents to her kingdom, where she sat the father on a golden throne, the mother on a silver throne and.....

The Fortune of an Old Shepherd

In olden times there lived an old shepherd, who worked for a rich farmer. It was his habit to throw stones into a hole, that lay on the way to the grazing grounds.

"Old shepherd, what is it that you want from me that you should knock on my door every day?" said a mole, who came out of the hole one day.

"I'm sorry, I didn't mean anything."

"Then, please stop knocking on my door every day. If you do I will give you whatever you want."

"In that case, what I would like is the power to understand the languages of all the animals in the world."

"I see, then you shall indeed have the power," said the mole.

No sooner had the mole spoken than he began to understand the chirping of the birds in the nearby trees and the bleating of his sheep. Even with this special knowledge he continued to be a shepherd. He listened to the birds in the trees and to the sheep's worries about their impending death.

It so happened that soon afterwards the farmer decided to kill a fat ewe, who had a very young lamb. She came to know about her master's decision and sadly, her fleecy cheeks wet with tears, she called the lamb to give him her last advice: "I will be killed tomorrow, so you'll have to look after yourself now. You should never go at the head of the flock, because you will be eaten by a fox, nor at the end of the flock because you will be often hit by stones from the shepherd's sling. Also you should always sleep in our usual place, because underneath the ground there is a piece of gold, which will keep you warm through the cold winter nights."

Immediately after she had spoken these words the shepherd went to the place and dug in the earth, where he found a piece of shining gold. He pocketed it quickly and ran away, taking the two sheep with him.

Tired and hungry, they spent the first night under a tree, on top of which a pair of crows and a pair of vultures had built their nests. The father crow came home very late at night and the mother crow asked him why.

"The Prince is very sick with some bees nesting in his ear and people were offering prayers for his recovery. I waited on the palace roof hoping for some *tormas*, but they did not throw any. I felt very hungry and swallowed something solid that I found on the way which has given me a terrible stomach-ache."

"There is nothing very seriously wrong with the Prince," said the father vulture, "he can be cured very easily by placing flowers on his head and milk and water below his ear."

The father crow was in excruciating pain as he listened to what the vulture said. He writhed in agony and losing his balance, fell on the ground, where he died. The shepherd opened the crow's stomach to see what had caused him so much pain and found another piece of shining gold.

The mother crow cried and lamented the loss of her husband throughout the night. Although the vulture couple tried hard to console her, she would not stop crying, and neither the vultures nor the shepherd could sleep.

Listening sympathetically to the mother crow, the shepherd kept on thinking of the sick prince. He imagined how rich he would be, when the King rewarded him for curing the Prince.

The next morning, when the birds left their nests early in search of food, he started on his journey towards the palace with the two sheep trailing lazily behind him. He came across a galloping horseman, with a foal trotting behind. The foal called to his mother to wait for him.

"I have no time to wait for you, when your dear Prince is about to die," replied the mother. "What's more, a needle in this saddle is pricking me in the back and causing me a lot of pain."

Immediately, the shepherd called the horseman to stop and took the needle out of the saddle.

"If you are so clever that you know about things that are hidden," said the horseman. "Perhaps you can also cure our Prince."

He agreed to cure the Prince and mounting the horse behind the horseman, they rode together to the palace.

The King and Queen and all the ministers were waiting for him with ceremonial gifts and took him to see the sick Prince. Once he was with the Prince he asked for paper of different colours, water and milk to be brought and asked that nobody disturb him for three days.

When he was alone he pretended to recite an unending series of prayers and rituals. On the third day he made many colourful paper flowers and placed them on the Prince's head, then he placed a pot full of milk and another of water below his ear. After arranging these things in this way, it happened that a baby bee came flying out and saw the flowers and water. He quickly went back in and told his mother that it was already summer time outside and they should change their nest. He told her of the beautiful flowers and cool springs that had formed outside their nest. The mother bee lost no time in leaving, and the Prince soon became well.

When the shepherd opened the door of the Prince's room, he invited the King and Queen and all the others to see the recuperating Prince and how much he had improved.

The King and the Queen were overjoyed to see their Prince well again. They thought that the shepherd was indeed some special doctor and rewarded him so lavishly that in his contentment, he forgot all about his two sheep and even the two shining pieces of gold.

A Witty Bride for Lonpo Gar's Son

Lonpo Gar Tongtsen was a minister of King Songtsen Gampo, the 32nd King of Tibet. He was popularly known as Lonpo Gar, and was notorious for his shrewdness. He outwitted all the other ministers in everything they did. In fact, he was so clever, no one could compete with him.

Ever since his son had grown up, his future had been a source of constant worry for *Lonpo* Gar. One day he thought, "My son is not very bright; I must find him a nice, clever wife." However, despite his cleverness and the great efforts he went to, he was unable to find a suitable wife for his son. So one day he gave the son a hundred rams and said, "You are not to kill or sell them, but must bring the rams back with one hundred bags of barley, or else I will not allow you to enter my house," and with that he sent him away.

The son went to town, but he had no money to buy so many bags of barley. Far from getting a hundred bags, he could not even think of how to get one bag. He sat down at the fair end of town pondering the problem, but no solution came to mind. He was getting very depressed when, all of a sudden, a fair young lady appeared before him.

"What is the matter, that you are so depressed?" she asked.

He related his sad story to her.

"There is no need to feel so sad about it, I can think of a solution." So saying, she sheared the rams of their wool and sold it. With the proceeds she bought a hundred bags of barley and sent him home, very cheerful.

He expected his father to be pleased with him. But when he got home and told his father of his experience, his father was not interested in listening to his adventure.

The very next day, *Lonpo* Gar called his son again and told him, "Last time you sheared all the fleece, which was not at all acceptable to me. Tomorrow you will take those hundred rams again and come back with a hundred bags of barley as before, otherwise you will not be allowed to return home." With these words *Lonpo* Gar sent his son away again.

Forlorn and without hope, he went to the same town as before and sat thinking at the far end of it, hoping that the girl would again come to his rescue.

Just as he had hoped, the girl came and sat beside him and again asked him the reason for his gloom. He poured out his grievances to her and said, "Since there is no more wool to be sheared, I cannot buy any barley at all, and my father will not allow me to return home."

The girl thought for a while and said, "Why can't you? Where there's a will, there's a way." She cut off all the horns, made knife and tool handles from them and sold them in the market. With the money obtained she bought barley, loaded the hundred rams and bade him farewell once more.

Victoriously, he went home and displayed the hundred bags of barley before his father. When his father saw the rams without their horns, he asked him who had taught him all these tricks, so the boy told him the whole story.

"Go and tell the girl that if she is so clever, she must make a nine arm-spans length of rope from ash and bring it to me," said his father.

He went and repeated his father's message to the girl, who replied, "Ask your father if he is willing to wear the rope around his neck after I have made it."

He went and conveyed the girl's counter challenge to his father. *Lonpo* Gar thought that it was impossible to make such a rope and promised to wear it. The next day, the girl laid a nine arm-spans length of rope on a slab of stone and burnt it. Now she had the rope ready, completely made of ash! She took it to *Lonpo* Gar and asked him to wear it. He was not only amazed to see the rope, but also ashamed that he was unable to put it around his neck.

Lonpo Gar was impressed by the girl's talent and cleverness and without a second thought, he married her to his not-too-clever son. At last, he had managed to find him a suitable bride.

Ribong Shoto (Cleft-Lipped Hare)

This is an anecdote explaining how the hare got its cleft lip. A good number of years ago a hare, wolf, fox and a raven got together and decided that robbery was the most adventurous and easiest way of living. For many days they could not bag anything until, finally, they saw a lone pilgrim with a great load of luggage on his back coming in their direction.

As soon as they saw him each of them went to play their own part: the fox lay down near the bank of the river and pretended to be dead, the hare and the wolf hid behind a rock, while the raven squarked, flew here and there and drew the attention of the pilgrim towards the fox. When the pilgrim saw the fox he thought that the skin would make a warm cap for himself or that he could sell the fur for a good price in Lhasa. He left his baggage by the roadside and hurried towards the fox but, as he approached, the fox jumped up and ran off, and he followed it in lame pursuit. Meanwhile, the hare and the wolf had stolen the baggage and retreated to their hideout.

Back in their hideout the four accomplices eagerly opened the baggage. They found a Chinese shoe, a rosary, a small bell and lots of *tsog* and *torma*. They quarrelled amongst themselves over the privilege of dividing the loot. Each claimed that they should be given the privilege, for the special efforts they had put into stealing them.

"Since I am the oldest among us, the privilege of dividing the goods falls to me," said the hare, and they all agreed without further complaint or protest. He gave the shoe to the wolf and told him that it would be useful when chasing sheep. The rosary, he gave to the raven and advised him to wear it around his neck when asking for food from the nomads. "They will say 'a heavenly bird has landed on our tent' and give you a lot of *tsog* and *torma*," he said. He gave the small bell to the fox and advised her to ring it to stop her children from crying. He, himself, took all the *tsog* and *torma*, and the four friends parted company.

The next day the wolf, the fox and the raven met together. "The hare has cheated me," said the wolf. "When I went to catch a sheep, the dogs and the villagers heard the noise of my shoe. They chased me and, when I tried to run, I stumbled and fell. They caught me and almost beat me to death. Now I shall kill the hare."

"Same with me," complained the raven. "I wore the rosary around my neck and squarked on the nomads' tent. The children heard me and they pelted me with stones, and when I tried to fly away, the rosary got entangled with the tent pole. They caught me and almost killed me. I wished I were dead rather than suffer at their hands. I must do something about the hare."

The fox too had suffered no less. "I rang the bell to stop my children from crying, but they fainted and died. That idiotic hare has fooled me. I will not leave without taking revenge on him. Either he dies or I die; only one of us can remain alive."

Having had their say and willed themselves to take revenge on the hare, they went in search of him.

Being guilty, the hare knew as soon as he saw them that they had come to fight him. He was left with no escape. Quickly, he picked up a sharp stone and cut his lip with it, then went to meet them.

"What has happened to your lip?" they asked in unison when they saw the deep wound.

"Oh, it was very bad. I think that man was a black magician. He has put a heavy curse on the *tsog* and *torma*. When I ate them my lip got terribly cut. I hope none of you experienced anything as unfortunate as this."

"Oh no, nothing happened to us. We are sorry to see you in such a plight," they said. And they went away cheated for the second time.

The hare was able to avoid their attack, but the mark of his cut lip remained forever, becoming a hereditary mark of all the hares-to-come.

King Kyaga Gyalpo

Once upon a time there was a king named Kyaga Gyalpo. Of his many servants, two were a mother and her son.

"Mother, mother, last night I had a very strange dream of succeeding to our King's throne," said the son one day.

The mother hushed him and warned him not to tell anyone else about it, lest the King should come to hear of it and punish them, or even expel them from his service.

But the mother herself was very talkative and curious to know if the dream could be interpreted. She went about asking all the other servants, but received no reply from them. Needless to say, the news of the boy's dream soon reached the King's ear.

He summoned the boy and, as a punishment for his bold dream, made him put on a pair of iron shoes and ordered him into exile, telling him to return only when the soles were completely worn out.

Wearing the heavy iron shoes he wandered from place to place for many days until he came to a lake. Completely exhausted with hunger and thirst, he sat down by the lake and studied the soles of the shoes to see if there was any sign of them wearing out in the near future. To his dismay, he found that the soles were as new as when he was first ordered to wear them. And, since he could not return home before they were worn out, he thought that he would never see his mother again.

While he was lost in these sad thoughts, a white and a black snake emerged from the lake and on seeing each other, flew into a fierce writhing fight. After a while, the white snake was wounded and just as the black snake was about to kill him, the boy flung one of his shoes and killed the black snake. Immediately, an eagle landed nearby, who put the white snake in a hat and flew away with the dead black snake.

While the boy was wondering about these events and nursing the wounded snake, seven black horsemen appeared out of the lake and asked him if he had seen a black snake. When he told them that an eagle had flown away with it, they galloped off after the eagle. Next, seven white horsemen followed them out of the lake and asked if he had seen a white snake promising to repay his kindness if he could help them. He showed them the white snake in the hat, and asked if it was the one they were looking for. They said it was, that he was their Prince and thanked him for saving his life. They invited him to their underwater realm, the land of the *nāgās*. But he declined fearing that he would drown in the water. They assured him that it was not very difficult to reach there and told him to close his eyes, while they put him on a horse and entered the lake. He did not have to keep his eyes closed for long, before he was asked to open them again. He found himself in the realm of *nāgās* standing before a magnificent palace, the like of which he had never seen or dreamt of before.

He was welcomed by beautiful *nāgā* boys and girls with flowers, milk, honey and a vast array of delicious dishes. He was entertained by music of the violin and many other melodious instruments peculiar to the kingdom. Every day during his stay there, he dropped the left-overs of his food into a small hole that he found in his room.

One day an old woman emerged from the hole, with a lock on her mouth, which she begged him to open. When he did so, she said, "You have been very kind to me in giving me food, otherwise I would have died of hunger. I am a servant here but because of my talkativeness this lock was put on my mouth and I was imprisoned below your room. Now, in return for your kindness, I have three pieces of advice: do not stay here long, and when you leave here do not take any of the precious stones you will be offered, ask only for a dog, a zebra and a blanket." She then returned to her cell.

The next day, despite repeated requests to stay longer, he announced his wish to leave. He was offered the most valuable gems, but he declined to accept them and asked instead for a dog, a zebra and a blanket as the old woman had advised. Although these were the *nāgās'* most cherished possessions, because the boy had saved his life, the Prince ordered these things to be given to him. The Prince then brought him to the edge of the lake where they had first met.

Alone, with nothing to do and nowhere to go, he first set up an improvised tent with the zebra as the pole and the blanket hung over it. Then tying the dog nearby he went off to explore the wilderness.

In the evening, he returned to find that in place of his improvised tent, there was an enormous marquee with his own dog at the entrance. He went inside and found bags and bags of grain. In the centre stood a huge stove with food prepared on it, but there was no one to be seen. He waited for a while, but nobody arrived, so he ate some food and went to sleep.

In the morning when he woke up he found everything ready for him; water fetched and food prepared but, still, there was nobody in sight. After eating some food he left to explore the wilderness further. When he returned in the evening he found food prepared and everything ready for him, as in the morning and the night before. This went on for some days.

He grew more and more anxious to find out who was doing all this work for him. So, one morning, he pretended to leave and hid behind the marquee. A little later the dog shed its skin and an enchantingly beautiful girl appeared. She washed the dishes, prepared food and went to fetch water. While she was away he threw the dog skin onto the fire and burnt it. Soon she returned with a pail full of water. When she saw him she asked him why he had returned earlier than usual. Wanting to revert to her dog form, she looked for the skin but could not find it. She asked him if he had seen it, and he told her that he had burnt it so that they could be together for the rest of their lives.

Instead of being happy she was very concerned, saying that he had committed a grave error in burning the skin and that there was no way to bring it back. She gathered up the ashes of the skin and scattered them all over the hill praying:

"May the top of the hill be covered with horses, the middle with wealth and the bottom with sheep."

Her prayers were answered instantly. They lived in perfect happiness for some time, but somehow he was not satisfied. He wanted to show his wealth to the other people; he wanted everybody to see his prosperity.

"Now that we are rich and happy, why not invite King Kyaga Gyalpo to a feast?" he remarked one day.

She told him not to do so, as it would only bring them unhappiness, but he could foresee no unhappiness in merely inviting the King. He insisted and she had to consent, but on the condition that he would not ask her to serve too frequently during the feast, to which he agreed. So, they invited not only the King, but also his ministers.

On the day of the feast she put soot on her face to conceal her beauty. When the King and his ministers arrived, he took them around to show his wealth and prosperity. They were surprised and showered jealous praise upon him. Highly pleased by their flattery, he ordered the girl to bring tea, food, *chang*, and other delicacies which took his fancy, regardless of what she had told him.

In her fatigue drops of sweat rolled down her face and washed the soot away. Suddenly the whole area was filled with the radiance of her beauty and everybody looked in awe, for they had never even dreamt of such beauty. Immediately the King expressed his desire to take the girl as his queen. The boy offered to give him any of his treasures, except the girl. The King replied that they should have a contest and that the winner would take the girl.

The following day the King said, "We will pour curd on the top of the hill tomorrow morning and the one whose curd reaches the base of the hill first will take the girl."

For the purpose of this contest the King imposed a tax on his subjects that every man should bring a barrel of curd and he had a sea of it at his disposal. He was so confident that he would win the girl, that he had even had dresses and jewellery brought for the girl and ordered his ministers to make preparations for the wedding.

When the boy heard the King's proposal, he knew that he would lose the contest and never see the girl again. He regretted burning the dog skin, inviting the King and over-working the girl during the feast. He went home and told her about the contest, but she was helpless because he had paid no heed to her advice. She told him that the only thing to do was to ask the help of the *nāgās*, whose Prince he had saved.

The next morning he set out early for the lake and called from the shore, "The biggest leather-bag of curd is too heavy; the smallest, not enough; give me the medium-sized bag." After calling continuously for some time a leather-bag of curd appeared out of the lake. He took it with him to the top of the hill, where he found that the King's curd had already reached halfway down the hill. He felt that he had already lost his dear girl. However, as soon as he opened the bag of curd, it flowed swiftly down the hill and reached the base first.

"You are the winner today," said the King, "but tomorrow we shall have another contest: we will scatter two measures of oil-seeds on the ground and the one who picks up his share first will take the girl." Unhappy once again, he went home. The girl consoled him and told him to go and ask the *nāgās* for the medium-sized box.

As he had done the day before, he set out early for the lake and called to the *nāgās*: "I cannot carry the biggest box; the smallest is too small; give me the medium-sized one." After a few calls a box appeared out of the lake.

He took it and went to enter the contest. On the way he wondered what could be inside such a small box that could help him pick up the seeds. He opened it and out flew a flock of pigeons, leaving only a broken-winged one behind. With that he went on to the contest. There he set the pigeon on the ground to pick up the seeds, while he sat aside, musing. Although the King had assembled all his subjects to help him in the contest, the boy once again defeated them all.

Defeated a second time, the King felt very ashamed and returned to his palace without casting so much as a glance at the boy or the girl.

The boy went home and related the story of his victory to the girl.

"Waste no time," she said. "Go and ask the *nāgās* to help you for the last time. Ask them to give you the *mag-gam.*"

As the girl had instructed, he obtained the mag-gam from the *nāgās*. They took it together to the king's palace and opened it before him. Out rushed many elfish-looking, iron-clad soldiers shouting; "Whom to strike, where to strike?"

"Strike Kyaga Gyalpo's head and neck," the boy and the girl replied.

Before he could escape the soldiers charged at the King, struck his head and neck and killed him.

With Kyaga Gyalpo dead, the boy's strange dream of taking over the King's throne became a reality. He became the King and the girl his Queen. Prosperity, happiness and all good things abounded thereafter.

The Frog who Married the Princess

One day an old woman was washing her feet, when a frog popped out of her calf. She felt so angry and upset that she should have given birth to a frog, rather than a human being and, also that it should have come out of her calf. She wanted to kill it.

"Please do not kill me," begged the frog, "I will work for you and repay your kindness."

Though she felt that a frog could be of no service to her, she spared its life.

For many days the frog worked for the old woman. He fetched water, collected wood and cooked for her. He truly repaid the old woman for sparing his life, and the old woman was happy that she did not have to do any work, but could just eat, sleep and say her daily prayers.

"I have worked hard to repay your kindness, now I have another request to make", said the frog one day.

"What is it that you want me to do?" asked the old woman.

"Now that I have grown up a lot, I want to marry the Princess."

"But you are a frog, the King would never give you his only daughter."

But the frog insisted and went to the palace himself, where he shouted at the gate: "Your majesty, please give me your daughter to be my wife."

"Begone, you old frog, I will not give my daughter to be your wife," retorted the Queen.

"Right then, I'll leave," said the frog, but as he walked, the whole palace shook with strong tremors.

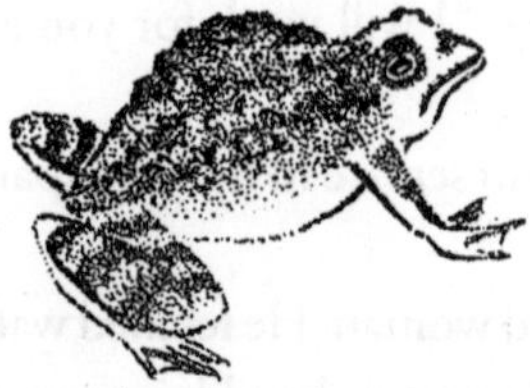

The Queen begged him not to go and promised to do whatever he asked. But when he again asked for the Princess, she would not give in.

"If you don't keep your word and give me your daughter, I am going to cry."

"Who cares if you cry?" answered the Queen. "Go ahead and cry as much as you want."

The frog cried and soon the whole palace was flooded with water. When the Queen begged him to stop crying, promising that she would give him the Princess, the frog stopped and the water disappeared. Then the Queen took back her promise.

"If you don't give me your daughter I will laugh," the frog threatened, "but it won't be an ordinary laugh."

"You may laugh till your lungs burst, but I will not give you my daughter."

He laughed a little and the whole palace cracked. Though the Queen cried and begged him to stop laughing, he would not do so unless both she and the King pledged to give their daughter to him as his wife. Eventually, they gave their pledge and kept to it at last.

Escorting the Princess and hopping with joy and excitement, he returned home and asked the old woman to open the door.

"You can come in through the crack," she called.

"I can come through the crack, but what about the Princess?"

The old woman opened the door and found that the frog had really brought the Princess home to be his wife. When the old woman asked him how he had managed to persuade the King and Queen to give him the Princess, he told her how many times he had begged them and how many times he had been cheated. "But you know, I am so young and handsome that the King and the Queen finally gave me the Princess," he concluded.

Once he was married he was busier than before. He worked dutifully for the old woman, but at the same time took great care of his dear wife. The old woman was happy, because the frog did her work for her and the Princess talked to her and kept her company. The Princess was happy, because the frog was a devoted husband and the old woman was very kind to her. But the frog was the happiest of all, because the princess was his wife.

They lived happily for some time. But, one day, when the frog went out to fetch water, a raven flew off with him. He shouted to the old woman and his wife for help, but they could do nothing else but stare, and cry for help themselves.

"If he lands down there on that grassy place I will be in luck, for I'll be able to meet my father," the frog croaked to himself.

The raven heard this and immediately climbed higher into the sky and looked for another place to land and eat the frog. Finding nowhere suitable, he thought that the roof of a house would be the next best place. The frog knew the raven's intention and said to himself, "How nice it will be for me, if he lands on that roof? I will be able to meet my uncle, whom I haven't seen for many years."

When the raven heard this he was afraid that the frog's uncle would come to his rescue and he would thus lose his meal. Higher and higher he climbed, as he looked for a suitable place to eat the frog, when he heard him mutter, "It will be miserable for me, if he lands on the bank of the river and eats me. I won't be able to meet any of my relatives before I die."

Immediately, the raven swooped down and landed on the bank of the river. He dropped the frog on the ground and sat on him, while he rested after his long flight. The frog begged the raven not to sit on him, saying that he had some good advice to give him.

"I know you are going to eat me and I am ready to submit to you, but you know, my skin is very hard, so it is advisable that you sharpen your beak on that stone, while I wait for you here."

The raven thought that the frog was right and went to sharpen his beak. While he was sharpening it the frog jumped, plop, into the river and disappeared. He swam across the river and overcame many other obstacles, before he finally reached home, to the delight of the old woman and his dear, dear wife.

Sha-Pho-Pho and Tsil-Lug-Lug
(Meaty & Fatty)

This is a Tibetan story explaining how vultures received the white mark on their heads.

Once there was a man named Sha-Pho-Pho and his faithful wife, Tsil-Lug-Lug. It had long been their custom for Sha-Pho-Pho to tend to their flock of sheep, while Tsil-Lug-Lug stayed at home and did all the housework. They divided their tasks so evenly between them, that there was not a single occasion when one accused the other of having done nothing. They were not very rich, but they were very happy.

Every day, when Sha-Pho-Pho returned home in the evening with the sheep, Tsil-Lug-Lug gave him lot of greasy soup to drink, and he steadily grew fatter, but not as fat as Tsil-Lug-Lug. He did not know how or from where she got so much oil and was anxious to discover her source, but he never actually asked her. He thought it would not be very difficult to find the truth and waited.

One day he pretended to leave with the sheep, but hid behind the house and peeped in through the window. After a while Tsil-Lug-Lug heated a huge metal pan over the stove, undressed herself and rolled three times in it. When she got out, the pan was filled with oil. Sha-Pho-Pho watched and thought, "If she can produce oil that way, why can't I? There is no difference between us."

The next day he insisted that she go out and look after the sheep and that he would stay at home and do the housework. She tried to dissuade him, saying that he would not be able to do all the work, but he would not listen to her. So, she went out to look after the sheep and he stayed home. After she had gone, he quickly heated the pan, took off his clothes and jumped into it. But poor Sha-Pho-Pho had no fat to melt—he was not as fat as his wife—and he was roasted to death in the pan.

In the evening when Tsil-Lug-Lug returned and found her beloved husband, Sha-Pho-Pho, dead in the pan she knew that he had imitated her and realised why he had insisted on staying at home that day. In tears, she went to look for a monk to conduct the funeral ceremonies.

On the way she met a pigeon, who asked her where she was going so much in tears. She cried that her husband had died and she was looking for a monk to perform the funeral ceremonies.

"How lucky you are! I am a monk," said the pigeon.

"If you are a monk, utter one word to prove yourself," said Tsil-Lug-Lug, and the pigeon muttered "mug mug mug mug."

"You are not a monk," said Tsil-Lug-Lug, and went on her way.

Then she met a magpie, who also asked her where she was going. When she told him that she was looking for a monk to perform the funeral ceremonies, the magpie said, "If you are looking for a monk to perform the ceremonies, I am not only a monk but I can also perform the ceremonies."

Tsil-Lug-Lug told him to say one word as proof, and the magpie croaked, "ka ka ka ka", but Tsil-Lug-Lug was not satisfied and went on her way.

Then she met a raven, who asked her the same question, and claimed that he was a monk. When Tsil-Lug-Lug made him say a word in proof, the raven squarked "caw caw caw caw", and she found out that he was not a monk and she went on her way.

Next she met a vulture and when he asked her where she was going, she related her sad story to him.

"Oh, how sad it is, would it be all right if I come with you?" asked the vulture.

"First you must give me one word to prove that you can be of any help to me," said Tsil-Lug-Lug.

The vulture was very clever and remembered the few words that he had learnt during the course of his many visits to the corpse-chopping grounds.

"*Chom-den de, De-zhin Sheg-pa,*" uttered the vulture.

When she heard him speak these words, she did not ask him to prove himself a second time. She had no doubt of his usefulness and happily invited him to her house to perform the funeral ceremonies.

As soon as they reached the house, she seated the vulture on a high cushion and placed the body of her husband in front of him. She then went to prepare some food for him. She was very sad that her husband was dead, yet so excited to have found someone reliable to perform the ceremonies, that she had forgotten to give the vulture any instructions. When she came back with a pot of curd for him, he asked her to bring the body of her husband.

"I placed it before you, *lama-la*," said Tsil-Lug-Lug.

"Oh, what a pity," said the vulture, "I thought that was the reception meal and ate it up."

Tsil-Lug-Lug was furious but could not do anything about it. She just threw the pot of curd at the vulture's head and dismissed him.

Poor Tsil-Lug-Lug cried for ever more and the vulture went away without performing the funeral ceremonies, but with his stomach full to the brim and a white mark on his head.

The Old Ogre

In ancient times there were many devils in Tibet. They roamed freely in the forests and mountains, but did no harm to the meditators in retreat there. But, they were a nuisance to the shepherds, who had to keep a constant watch on them to prevent any of them walking off with a sheep.

Among these devils was one very ferocious, old ogre, of whom everyone was very afraid; even the other ogres were afraid of him. He not only stole sheep, but also human children and ate them in his cave. When he had nothing else to eat, he would go to one of the other ogres and snatch away his day's catch. In this way he was a bully to the other ogres and an object of constant fear to the villagers.

At the end of the village there lived an old woman and her daughter. They had no neighbours to talk to, or to ask for help, but they were very happy with their simple, isolated life. They were also happy because, though many other families had lost their children to the old ogre, they had not been visited by him at all. Every morning and evening the mother thanked the gods for the protection given to them so far and prayed for further protection.

One day the mother called her daughter to her and warned, "Do not open the door to anyone until I come back, otherwise the old ogre will come and take you away," and she went out to pick *doma*.

Just as her mother had instructed, the girl closed the door and the windows tightly and stayed inside. But after a short time, there came a knock on the door.

"Who is it?" the girl asked. "My mother told me not to open the door to anyone until she returned."

"Why, I am your mother," came the reply.

"If you are my mother, show me your hands through the hole in the door."

When a very big, hairy hand appeared through the hole, she exclaimed, "These are not my mother's hands. Her hands are smooth and yours are hairy."

"It's all right if you don't want to open the door, but will you please give me some oil and some fire?"

The girl quickly gave him some oil and fire thinking that he would go away. But instead, he rubbed the oil on his hands and burnt off the hair. Then coming back to the door, he called, "Daughter, open the door. I am your mother."

"Your voice does not sound like my mother's, but anyway show me your hands."

When she saw the smooth hands, the girl opened the door; seeing that it was not her mother but the old ogre himself, she ran and hid behind a beam in the ceiling. He searched everywhere. He searched for her in the barrels, under the beds and in every corner, but could not find her. He was so tired, that he let off a booming fart and the girl gave a great shriek of laughter. Then he found out where she was and tried to reach her, but could not do so. He asked her how she got up there.

"I piled needles upon needles and climbed up," she said.

So he piled needles upon needles but could not climb up. He threatened that she should speak the truth or he would smash her body into pieces and devour her.

"I piled *phorpas* over *phorpas* and climbed up," she said, but he could not climb the pile of *phorpas*. This time he threatened her even more strongly and said that he would devour her alive if she did not tell him the truth. She was very scared and told him that she had piled barrels on top of barrels and climbed up. So he piled barrels on top of each other and climbed up and seized her and took her to his cave.

In the evening when the mother returned, she found her daughter missing and learnt that the old ogre had taken her away. She was very sad that her only source of happiness and comfort was gone. So, she packed some *tsampa* in her *thangkuk* and went in search of her daughter.

On the way she met a raven, who asked her why she was crying and where she was going.

"My daughter has been taken away by the old ogre and I am going in search of her," she answered.

The raven asked for some *tsampa* and promised to help her in her search. She gave him some, and they went on together. Next they met a fox, who asked why the old woman was crying and where they were going. She told him about the old ogre and her daughter. He also asked for some *tsampa* and promised to accompany them in their search. She also gave him some *tsampa* and the three of them went on together.

Then they met a wolf and he too asked where they were going. When the old woman told him about her daughter's misfortune, he also asked for some *tsampa* and promised to help in rescuing her daughter. Gratefully, the old woman gave him some *tsampa* and the four of them went on together. As they were nearing the old ogre's cave, the wolf said, "We must make a plan to get the girl, otherwise we will also be devoured by the old ogre."

So, they made a plan and went right up to the old ogre's cave, which was like no other. It was very large with bones of different animals lying all around. Directly in front of the cave, they were surprised to find a big pen containing hundreds of sheep. It was the fox who was the first to give up the idea of rescuing the girl. He was not only afraid of the old ogre, but very much tempted by the number of helpless sheep waiting to be eaten. But the raven and the wolf threatened to kill him, if he did not help them as he had promised.

And, so, as they had planned earlier, the wolf went into the pen and ran here and there among the sheep, scaring them and throwing everything into chaos. Immediately, the old ogre came out of the cave and hurled a big stone at the wolf. The wolf pretended to be dead and the raven sat on him to show the old ogre that he really was dead. Thinking that he could eat the wolf later, the old ogre started to chase the fox away. As he ran faster and came closer, the fox increased his own speed and running as fast as the wind, swiftly disappeared into the forest.

Meanwhile, the wolf, the raven and the old woman entered the old ogre's cave and found the girl in a sack hanging over the fire-place. They rescued her, filled the sack with ice and thorns and fled.

When he failed to catch the fox, the old ogre returned to his cave and was very pleased to find that none of the sheep was missing, but he was still angry that the fox had cheated him and escaped. He was very tired from the chase and decided to eat the girl to reward himself. As he lit the fire to prepare his dinner, the ice melted.

"Girl, don't wet yourself," he cried, but the ice continued to melt. In his anger he grabbed the sack and was pricked by the thorns. He thought that the girl was angry and pinching him and, in a fit of pique, grabbed for her again, so the thorns pricked him even more. To his anger and dismay he found only ice and thorns in the sack and then realised that the fox, the raven, the old woman and the wolf had come not to steal his sheep, but to rescue the girl. He was absolutely furious and burned to take his revenge, especially on the fox, who had fooled him. So, he set out to find him.

When the fox saw the old ogre coming in his direction, with his fists raised and shouting abuse, he pretended to be winnowing sand.

The old ogre accused the fox of cheating him and swore that he would eat him on the spot.

"On that hill yonder live hundreds of foxes and over here hundreds more; there are one thousand, nine hundred foxes in all. I am 'the river-side sand-winnowing fox' and not the one you are looking for."

"Then will you teach me how to winnow sand?" asked the old ogre. The fox agreed and told him to lie down and open his mouth, nose and eyes. Pretending to winnow the sand, he stuffed the ogre's mouth, nose and eyes with it and ran off.

A little later the ogre caught up with him and growled, "What mischief you have done. You have stolen away the girl, stuffed my mouth, nose and eyes with sand and run away. This time I am not going to let you escape."

"What are you saying?" asked the fox. "On that hill yonder live hundreds of foxes and over here hundreds more foxes; one thousand, nine hundred foxes in all. I am 'the cliff-side glue-making fox' and not the one you are looking for."

The old ogre was convinced by the fox's words and forgot his anger in his keenness to learn the fox's art. He asked the fox to teach him the art of making glue and the fox agreed to do so. He smeared glue on a rock and made the old ogre close his eyes and sit on it. As he sat down, the fox smeared glue all over his face and again ran away.

The fox sat at the edge of a cliff and while appearing to be weaving a basket, he pretended not to see the old ogre coming towards him. Growling and swearing, the old ogre came up, threatening that he would eat him. He said, "There is nothing that you haven't done to me. You stole the girl, stuffed my mouth, nose and eyes with sand, glued my bottom to a rock and smeared my face with glue."

The fox replied, "On that hill yonder live hundreds of foxes and over here hundreds more foxes; there are one thousand, nine hundred foxes in all. I am 'the cliff-side basket-weaving fox' and not the one you are looking for."

"The same was said to me before, you must be the one I'm looking for." said the old ogre, but the fox insisted that he was not the one.

"In that case, will you teach me how to weave baskets?" the old ogre asked.

Pretending to teach him how to weave, he asked the old ogre to get inside a half-finished basket, while he continued to weave, slowly encasing the ogre. When it was finished the old ogre was safely enclosed and he could not get out. Laughing aloud the fox rolled him over the cliff and down into the river.

So, the scary, old ogre died at the hands of a small fox; the villagers thanked him heartily and lived in peace ever after.

The Ordeals of a Prince and a Princess

There were, once, two kingdoms of equal power and wealth, one on either side of a big river. They had been at peace with each other for many years and their people were free to move from one kingdom to the other. Now that the Kings were getting old, they were no longer interested in conquering each other and had entered into a lasting peace.

The King on the right side of the river had no son, but had been blessed with a beautiful, clever daughter, whose fame spread to far-off lands. She was very obedient to her parents and except when she went to circumambulate the stupa on full-moon nights, she remained indoors working and helping them. Many kings had climbed mountains and crossed rivers to seek her hand in marriage, but all had returned disappointed.

The King on the left side of the river had a son, who was not very clever, but was very kind-hearted. Since his childhood, his only dream had been to lead a religious life and he had never been interested in the throne or the affairs of the kingdom as were other princes, who were taught the arts of warfare and kingship from an early age. His ageing parents and their ministers were very disappointed in his attitude and were concerned that, if the lineage of succession to the throne were to be broken, the kingdom would face civil disorder and external invasion, once the King and Queen died.

Years went by before the King and Queen died. The ministers made hasty preparations to install the Prince on the throne and requested him to assume power. In spite of their earnest requests, he was reluctant and when he finally did agree to succeed his father to the throne, it was on condition that they find the girl, whose finger fitted his ring perfectly.

The ministers thought that it would be an easy task, but wasted no time. They searched all over their kingdom, but the ring fitted no one perfectly—it was either too small for some or too big for others. They reported their fruitless search to the Prince and asked him if they should dispatch men to other kingdoms in search of the right girl.

"Ha, ha, my faithful ministers, you have laboured hard and long," he laughed. "You need not have gone so far, because the right girl is just on the other side of the river."

Knowing the difficulties involved in getting this girl for him they wanted to dissuade him, but refrained lest he should revoke his earlier acceptance to be their new king. They thought it would be practically impossible to lure the Princess out of the palace to try the ring on her royal fingers. After a long discussion a few ministers finally volunteered to disguise themselves as rich merchants, to go to the other kingdom taking with them some lavish goods amongst which they would include the ring.

Right by the palace gate they displayed their merchandise and waited long and patiently for the Princess to come. When they were tired and on the verge of giving up, the Princess and the Queen came out to take a stroll on the palace roof and saw the ring shining brightly amidst the other things. The Princess came running down and asked them the price of the ring.

"I'm sorry, this ring is not for sale," a minister apologised, "we keep it only to improve the appearance of our goods, to attract people."

"Please sell it to me," she requested, "I will pay any price you ask."

"Well, before you buy it, please just try it on, as we wouldn't want you to pay for it if it didn't fit you."

She tried it on and it fitted so perfectly on her slender finger, it was as if it had been made for her, but when she tried to pull it off, it would not move at all.

"Please do not force it and hurt your finger. You can keep it today and pay for it tomorrow."

They quickly gathered their merchandise and returned to their own kingdom, where they related everything to the Prince, who was very pleased to hear the good news. Not only were the ministers talking eagerly amongst themselves, the Prince himself was very excited that the girl he loved would finally be his queen.

The next day the ministers approached the neighbouring King to persuade him to marry his only daughter to their Prince.

"How can we let her go?" asked the aged King and Queen. "She is our everything. If you can give us your Prince, we would be very happy with the marriage. We need someone like your Prince, so that our daughter may succeed to our throne."

"We are in an even greater dilemma. Our King and Queen have died and there is nobody but this Prince to succeed them. Without him on the throne, there will be chaos in the kingdom."

Both sides were reluctant to make any concessions and finally the ministers returned to their kingdom very disappointed. The Prince was even more depressed on hearing their distressing news.

Once again the ministers met together and concluded that the only way to win the King's compliance was to arrange for the Prince and the Princess to meet and thus lure the Princess to their side. Once they had stolen the heart of the Princess, they thought, it would not be difficult to gain the King's consent. The Prince also agreed to their proposal.

It was very easy to propose a meeting, but very difficult to arrange, as the Princess was in the habit of remaining constantly inside the palace. When they realised this, they sent men all over the other kingdom to find out if there were any means to achieve their aim. In this way they learnt that the only time for the Prince to meet the Princess would be on a full-moon night, when the Princess came to circumambulate the stupa.

It was arranged that the Prince would wait by the stupa on the night of the full-moon, but as night fell, the Prince was unable to keep his eyes open any longer and went to sleep. The Princess did her circumambulations, said her prayers and returned to the palace without noticing the sleeping Prince.

"No, I didn't meet the Princess because I fell asleep," the Prince told his eager ministers when they asked him about the meeting.

"This is very bad," they said. "It is a long wait till the next full-moon, but you must not miss her a second time. It is very important for you to stay awake."

When the next full-moon came, they sent the Prince to wait by the stupa and advised him to take some snuff to keep himself awake, but he fared no better this time, as he was again sound asleep when the Princess came and put a ceremonial scarf around his neck before she left.

Though the Prince had failed again, the ministers were hopeful and determined to try a third time, for they found some significance in the scarf that she had left for him.

When the third full-moon came, they instructed the Prince to take a good quantity of snuff to keep himself awake. Half dozing and half awake, the Prince managed not to sleep before the Princess came. His sleepy eyes opened wide on seeing her beautiful face, and the serene light of the moon added to her beauty. He told her that he had been waiting to meet her for the duration of three full-moons and expressed his only desire to marry her. She in return disclosed that it was her dream to be his queen. Since it was impossible for them to fulfill their dreams if they stayed in their own kingdoms, they decided to run away.

She returned to her palace and gathered a bundle of rich brocade and a few other things, while he did likewise. They met once again at the stupa and fled without thought of where they would go.

They walked the whole night on rugged roads and reached a thick forest in the morning. There they rested to eat the little food they had brought with them.

"You stay here and cook something, while I go and barter some of these things for food," said the Prince and went towards the nearby town.

He was gone a long while and in the meantime the King of that country saw smoke curling up from the middle of the forest. He dispatched five soldiers to arrest the unusual camper. They caught the Princess and took her with her things to the King. When he looked at her belongings he realised that she was not just an ordinary girl and confined her to the palace roof as a punishment for camping in his kingdom.

Meanwhile, the Prince had returned to the camp after selling and bartering most of their possessions, only to find the Princess gone. He knew that she would not deceive him and thought she could not have gone far.

In the hope of finding the Princess, he did not leave the kingdom, but went in search of her every day. She could see him from the roof, but could not do anything for fear of getting him arrested too. Whenever she threw a stone at him, he would always look sideways and not upwards, for he never imagined she was anywhere near the palace.

As the days went by, he had nothing left to sell and nothing to eat. He grew more and more ragged and later he looked so uncouth, that she could not believe he was her own beloved Prince. One day she threw a big stone at his head and called him. She told him who she was and threw down a big piece of gold, telling him to buy two horses and wait for her at the palace gate that night.

With the big piece of gold he bought the two best horses in the kingdom, a new *chupa* and ate a hearty meal to make up for all the days he had been hungry. He could already visualise himself and the Princess galloping away to freedom and assured himself that he would not have to pass through such hardship again.

That night, he tied the two horses near the gate and waited for the Princess to come. But, unfortunately, he could not stay awake for long and had fallen into a deep slumber, when two thieves happened to come by.

"Oh, here is a lucky turn for us," said one.

"Let us leave it and go ahead with our original plan," the other protested.

"No, no, let us see what happens. Looking at this boy waiting with two horses at the palace gate, I think we are going to earn a big fortune," he said and leading away one of the horses, they waited to see what would happen.

"Are you ready?" the Princess called after a while.

"Yes, I am ready," whispered one of the thieves.

She climbed down from the roof and rode off on one horse, followed by the thieves on the other. They rode as fast as the horses could carry them until daylight. When she discovered that she was not with her Prince but with thieves, the Princess was very distressed and pleaded with them to set her free.

The thieves paid no attention to her. No sooner were they off the horse than they quarrelled over possession of the girl. Each claimed that he had the right to keep her as his wife.

"There is no use quarrelling," she intervened. "I cannot belong to you both and quarrelling will bring no solution. The best thing will be for both of you to race from the foot of the hill back up to this point, and the winner shall be my husband.

They were happy to accept her suggestion and walked to the foot of the hill. As soon as they turned their backs, she galloped away on her horse and was soon out of their sight.

When they found the girl gone, they blamed each other for separating the boy and the girl and vowed to reunite them.

Meanwhile, the girl realised that she would not fare well dressed as a woman and disguising herself as a man, went in search of work. The first door she knocked on belonged to a rich farmer, who had only one daughter and a servant.

"Can you sweep?" the servant asked.

"I will be glad to accept any work you can give me."

They were very pleased with her and gave her work as the shepherd. In this she worked very hard and the sheep became fat and their numbers increased like never before. Then they asked her to look after the horses and she worked hard again.

One day the master called the Princess and said, "Son, we are thankful for your devoted service to us. Now, we do not want you to work like a servant, but to live happily with us as a member of the family. If you do not object, I would like you to marry my daughter."

Much as she wanted to explain that she was a girl not a boy, she could not, for fear that they would be angry with her for cheating them for so long. She was also afraid that once she was thrown out of the house, she would never see her beloved Prince again. She agreed to the farmer's proposal, and a lavish wedding ceremony was conducted.

A few days later, she approached the farmer to request his permission to build a temple.

"What is it that you wish me to do for you, son?" he asked.

"Please allow me to build a temple at the junction of the three roads that run in front of our house."

The farmer found no reason to refuse her request, as he himself was a very pious man, and he felt that a temple at the junction of the roads would be a better location than building it in a remote place.

When she had received his permission, she had a magnificent temple built, with facilities to offer free lodging to pilgrims. She then invited the best artist in the kingdom to paint a portrait of her, dressed as a woman, on one side of the wall. She also appointed a curator to look after the temple, giving him strict orders to report anyone making remarks about the portrait to her.

Many people came to pray and to make offerings, but nobody made any remarks about the portrait until, one day, five men came by.

"This looks like the whore," they remarked to each other.

The curator immediately reported this to the Princess, who had all five arrested. She recognised them as the five soldiers who had taken her away from the forest. She kept them imprisoned, but gave them nice food and treated them kindly.

Not many days later, two more men arrived and, as soon as they saw the portrait, one of them shouted, "Here she is!"

"Yes, it is her," the other agreed.

The curator reported this too, and the two men were also arrested and treated like the other five.

When she received no more reports for a long time, the Princess was very sad. She felt that her only chance of meeting the Prince again was lost. She was disheartened that the purpose of building the temple had not been realised, and thought it best to go in search of him.

One day an abjectly poor man in tattered clothes came staggering into the temple and begged for some food. The kind curator, who was very moved by his plight gave him some food and offered him work, sweeping, in exchange for food and shelter. The man accepted the offer gratefully and hungrily ate the food.

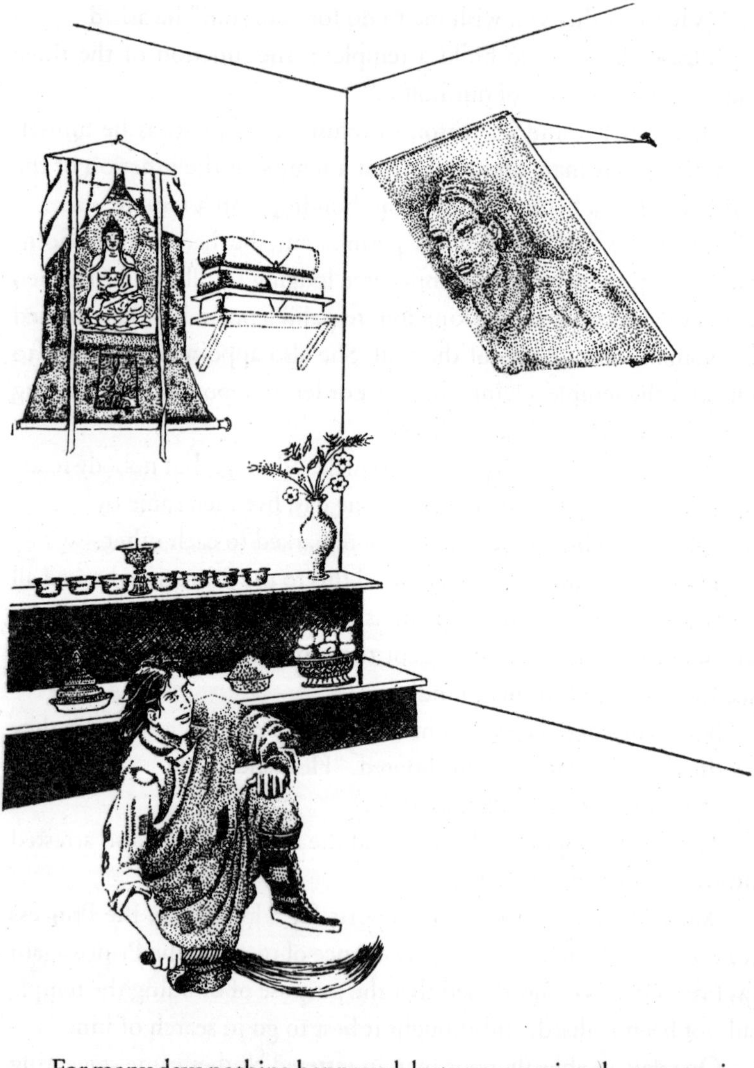

For many days nothing happened, but one morning the man noticed the portrait, as he stood up to take a breath from his sweeping. He stood there a long time with the broom in his hand, staring at it and shedding sorrowful tears. The curator asked him why he was crying.

"It's nothing, I am crying because of my miserable condition."

This went on for several days, so the curator was not convinced by the man's reply. He kept a check on him and discovered that he cried only in front of the portrait. Though the man made no direct remarks about the portrait, the curator thought that his behaviour was more significant than any remarks. When he reported it to the Princess, a ray of hope lit up her sorrowful heart. She directed the curator to bring the man to her and prayed silently that he was her beloved Prince.

When the curator brought the man to her, he begged her not to punish or imprison him as he would surely die. The man did not recognise the Princess dressed as a man and she could not imagine that her beloved had fallen into such a miserable state. She fainted at the very sight of him. When she regained consciousness, she quietly told him that she was the very Princess of his dreams. She had new clothes made for him, fed him and nursed his cracked skin. By and by, he came to believe that this kind boy was none other than his own beloved Princess in disguise, in search of whom he had travelled days and nights without food and water. He gradually regained his health and became as handsome as he had been in his days at the palace.

Finally, one day the Princess put on her women's clothes and went to see the farmer. She disclosed that she herself was a Princess and the man the Prince of a neighbouring kingdom. She related the whole story and aplogised for deceiving them. As proof of her story she named the seven men who had been imprisoned.

"If your honour wishes, both your daughter and I could marry this Prince," she suggested.

The farmer greatly admired her courage and her wisdom and was glad to arrange another wedding ceremony.

And so it was that the two girls were like two real sisters—faithful to each other and to their husband, and their family lived happily ever after.

The Thief and the Swindler

In the good old days when thefts were very rare and honesty an everyday thing, there was only one thief and one swindler in a certain village, who were both very good at their respective trades. They had each heard of the other, but had never met during their many years staying in this village.

The funniest thing was that both of them were married to the same woman. The reason they had never met each other, was that the thief was active at night and the swindler in the daytime. The thief left home as night fell and returned only at day break, while the swindler left at day break and returned only after dark. The wife never mentioned anything about her second husband to either of them. She was very faithful to both of them and each of them thought he was the happiest man in the whole kingdom, with a prosperous trade at hand and a faithful wife.

But they were not blessed to enjoy their happiness for long. It came to an end one day, when the King announced a reward for anyone who caught them or gave any news of their whereabouts.

"What to do?" the thief asked his wife one morning, "the King has ordered the arrests of me and the swindler. I don't care about the swindler, but I must urgently do something for myself."

"The safest thing is for you to stay away from this village for some time," she advised. She baked a big loaf of bread and cut it into two equal halves, wrapped them in two identical cloths and sent him away with one half.

He walked a long way, until he had to take refuge in a cave when it began to rain. He curled up in a corner to keep himself warm and chewed on the bread.

Back at the village, the swindler had also heard of the King's announcement and came running home, panting.

"What shall I do, my dear wife? The King has ordered my arrest."

"Don't worry," she said. "All that is necessary is for you to stay away from this village for some time and come back when everything quietens down again." She gave him the other half of the bread and sent him on his way.

Putting the bread in the pocket of his gown, he ran until he reached the cave where the thief was sheltering. He was very happy to find someone to spend the night with.

"What are you doing, friend?" he asked the thief.

"First tell me where you are going in such a hurry," the thief replied. Each of them was more anxious to know about the other, before disclosing his own identity, than to answer the other's questions. Finally the thief said, "We are friends and there is no reason for me to hide anything from you; I am the thief the King wants arrested."

"Then we are in the same boat," exclaimed the other, "I am the swindler the King wants arrested!"

"From now on we will travel together and share whatever we get," the thief suggested. He took out his bread and was about to share it with the swindler, when he was startled by the swindler's shout.

"Thief! You really are a thief. You've stolen my bread."

"No, friend, this is not your bread. It is my own bread, my wife baked it for me."

He was right; the swindler checked his pocket and found his bread still there. Both of them were amazed that two separate people should have the same type of bread in identical wrappings. They joined the two halves together and found that they formed a single whole. They then realised that they had both been sharing the same wife, and agreed that as they belonged to the same family, they should live together as they had before.

As night fell, the swindler said, "Friend, why don't you go and steal some food for us, I will earn something tomorrow."

After eating what the thief had brought, they went to sleep for the night and fell into a deep slumber, free from fears of arrest.

The next morning, the swindler rose early and went to an old woman pretending to be her own son.

"Oh, my poor old mother, how much I've missed you."

"What are you saying? I have no son, my only child is a daughter, but she is not here."

Because he was so insistent, the old woman accepted him as her own son and sent him to gather firewood and fetch the water.

"Mother, what is the most secret, guarded thing in this town?" he asked her.

"The marriage of the Governor's daughter is the most guarded secret of the town. They are not only afraid that bandits will attack them on their way to the wedding, but also because it is believed that the girl is an angel."

After buying three horses and a gun, he bid farewell to the old woman. On the day of the wedding he gave one horse to the thief and told him to wait behind two nearby hills. He dressed himself in expensive clothes and with the gun slung across his back, he rode to the ceremony with the spare horse richly saddled. He told the assembled guests that the girl's mother was very sick and that he had been sent to escort her home before her mother died. He quietly told the girl that it would not be good for her mother's health to take any more escorts and that it would be very inauspicious to visit her mother in her ordinary clothes and without her finest jewellery.

The way he was dressed and the great urgency of his manner, easily convinced the people and they hurriedly prepared the girl for departure. The swindler and the girl rode away until they reached where the thief was waiting for them. She then realised that she had been cheated, but there was nothing she could do.

"What do you want from me?" she asked them.

"We don't want anything from you and won't hurt you, if you cooperate with us in our business. After one month, we will return you safely to your parents."

Fearing that they would harm her if she did not cooperate, she promised to obey their orders. Riding further on, they came to another kingdom and pitched their tent in a beautiful, green garden. The garden was very sacred and the King did not even allow birds to enter it, let alone human beings. He used it himself only once a year to make the annual offerings to the gods.

When the King saw the tent pitched right in the middle of his sacred garden, he sent his treasurer to chase the intruders away. As the treasurer approached, the swindler gestured authoritatively that he should enter from the side and not from the front of the tent.

"The King has ordered you to leave this garden immediately," the treasurer commanded.

"Who is your King? We are from a powerful kingdom. The beauty of the Queen in this tent is famous in all four corners of the world. People have travelled for months on end, just to have a glimpse of her."

"Is that so, will you please allow me to have a look at her myself?"

"It is inauspicious to pay respects to such an honourable lady without bringing anything to offer her, but you may peep in at the side of the tent to satisfy yourself."

The treasurer was so excited by that mere glimpse of her, that he asked them to name the things he should bring, in order to obtain a proper, longer audience.

"You should bring rolls of brocade, some precious stones, tea and butter. It is confirmed that your audience will be at the first gun-fire this evening."

Instead of returning to the palace and informing the King of his findings, he went straight home and collected the things that he had been asked to bring and waited eagerly for the sound of gun-fire.

When the treasurer did not return, the King sent one of his ministers to chase the intruders away from his sacred garden. But he was also easily convinced of the lady's fame and after letting him have a brief glimpse of her, he was told to come with expensive presents at the second gun-fire for a longer audience. He also did not return to the King, but went straight home and made a large bundle of his most valuable possessions and waited.

Furious that neither the treasurer nor the minister had returned, the King himself went to chase the trespassers away from his sacred garden.

"How dare you pitch your tent in the middle of my sacred garden, when I have not even permitted birds to enter it? I have sent two messengers, but you have paid no heed to them."

"You may be a powerful King and this garden your sacred place, but the King that we represent is much more powerful. The lady in this tent is his Queen. Many kings have travelled for months and months with invaluable gifts just to have an audience with her, but you have the audacity to come here empty-handed. Aren't you ashamed of yourself?"

The King was not convinced of the existence of any such Queen in the tent and asked to see her.

"As a rich and powerful king it would be a disgrace to your honour, to approach her with nothing to offer, but if you insist on seeing her, we can allow you, as a king, to peep in through this opening in the door-flap."

The King was infatuated by her beauty, and the dress and jewellery she was wearing were enough to convince him of their story. He asked for a longer audience, and was told to come at the third gun-fire with presents worthy of his position and acceptable to a lady of her status.

When the King had gone, they told the girl that she would not have to stay with them for a month, for three days would be enough. They gave her instructions not to show any sign of sadness, nor to cry before the King, but to talk and behave like a real queen.

At the first gun-fire, the treasurer arrived with a huge load of presents and was ushered inside the tent for the audience. He was not ready to leave, when the minister arrived at the second gun-fire. He begged them to hide him somewhere, before the minister caught him. They hid him in a corner of the tent and covered him with a blanket.

The minister was not yet ready to go, when they heard the King approaching at the third gun-fire.

"Oh, it is only your King," they told him.

"Please hide me somewhere," he pleaded and they hid him under another blanket with a bowl on his head, right next to the treasurer.

The King was dressed in his best clothes and even had his crown on to impress the lady. They received the King and presented him to the girl. While the King was engrossed in talking admiringly to her, the swindler collected all the gifts the treasurer, the minister and the King had brought with them, and told the thief to ride off with them and wait some distance away.

After the thief had left, the swindler told the King that her highness wished to have a short break. He led the girl outside and they galloped off, in the direction that the thief was waiting.

The King waited a long time, hoping that the girl would return. The minister had been hiding so long, with the bowl balancing precariously on his head, that he felt very tired and shifting a little to change his position, he dropped the bowl from his head. The poor treasurer panicked at the unexpected noise and wet his pants. The King was no less shocked by the sound, because he thought he was the only person in the tent. He pulled away one blanket and found his own minister, who pulled away the other blanket, under which a puddle had formed and found the treasurer. They stared at each other in utter shame.

"It is a disgrace that we have all been deceived by those men because we were enchanted by a girl's beauty. To save our dignity it is best that we tell no one about this," said the King. So the three of them pledged total secrecy and returned to the palace.

Meanwhile, the thief and the swindler thanked the girl for her help and returned her safely to her home. Just between themselves, they promised not to engage in their trades any more. Richer than they had ever been before, they returned to their wife and lived happily together, till they died in ripe, old age.

The Frog and the Princess

Once upon a time, a King had three beautiful daughters, whom he loved as much as if he had three precious jewels. He wanted to find a suitable husband for each of them. Though many princes from various neighbouring kingdoms came to ask for their hands, the King did not find anyone suitable for his three lovely daughters. He was always afraid that he would die without having them married off. He feared that he would die an improper death without having fulfilled his duty as a father. Proud as he was, he was constantly worried about the future of his daughters.

An elderly childless couple, both well over sixty, worked as servants in the palace. Their lives were lonely and miserable.

One year, one of the old woman's knees became swollen. As she couldn't afford to see a doctor, the swelling grew so serious that she was hardly able to move an inch. When it burst, a big golden frog jumped out. Seeing this, the old man declared vehemently, "This frog must be an evil spirit. Throw that inauspicious thing away quickly!" The old woman didn't have the heart to get rid of it, so with tears in her eyes she persuaded him, saying, "Who knows whether he's an evil spirit or a monster, a god or a dragon? We have suffered bitterly for so long. Now we are old, yet we have no child to help us. Maybe God has shown us mercy and bestowed on us a frog instead of a son."

Fearing that his wife would grow more unhappy, the old man did not insist and let her have her way. Even so the old man felt disgusted whenever he caught sight of the ugly creature with its flat head, big mouth and a pair of protruding eyes. He left home in anger and disgust. From then on the frog became the old woman's only companion and even ate the same food she did. Every day the old woman would carry him in and out, treating him as if he were a baby. The little frog, though unable to speak, always opened his eyes wide as if he understood her kindness perfectly.

One day the old woman held the frog in her arms, teasing him, "Little frog, how nice it would be if you could talk!" The little frog's eyes bulged and he cried, "Mummy, Mummy, don't be sad. When I grow up I'll get married, and my wife will help you with everything and you won't have to work for the King any more." The old woman was so startled at hearing this that she almost dropped the little creature on the ground. She had never dreamed he could speak, let alone so thoughtfully. From then on, she cherished her little frog even more.

After a period of time, the little frog said to the old woman, "Mummy, it's high time you had a daughter-in-law to help you! Will you go and arrange the match?" The old woman asked, "But where can I go? Who would like to be the wife of a little frog like you! What's more, we are so poor." The little frog replied, "Don't worry! Go and ask to see the King and tell him, 'Your Majesty, haven't you got three princesses? Please can I have one for my daughter-in-law?" He will certainly agree. Then she can help you with your housework, can't she?"

The old woman laughed, "Little frog, what a sense of humour you have! How can a princess marry into a poor family like ours and what's more with a frog?" The little frog went on pleading, "Mummy! Mummy! Go and try, just once!" Seeing that he was in earnest, the old woman found it difficult to refuse him and so decided to try her luck.

When she came before the King, the old woman fell to her knees, saying, "Your Majesty, I have a request." The King asked, "What's the matter? No food, no clothes?" The old woman replied, "Thanks to your generosity, we have both. I've come to ask for a wife for my son. You have three daughters, please may one of them marry my son?"

No sooner had the old woman finished her explanation, than the King burst out laughing. "This old woman must be crazy or delirious. How can she talk such nonsense? Let my daughter become her son's wife? Impossible!" He gestured to his bodyguard and ordered, "Throw this mad old woman out!"

Driven out of the palace, she staggered homeward, complaining about the little frog all the way. As soon as she saw him, she cursed, "You little idiot! You don't know what's good and what's bad. You made me go and ask for trouble. There's an old saying: The peacock and the crow never fly together; the elephant and the ox can't get along with each other. Later you'll understand more and not have such fancy ideas."

Without waiting for her to finish grumbling, the little frog sprang up high in the air and shouted, "How can that be! I must go there by myself. Whether they agree or not, I'll marry one of the princesses. Just get your home ready to receive your daughter-in-law!" The little frog hopped to the gate of the palace and yelled, "Hey! King, ministers, officials, listen! I'm the son of the old woman who carries water for the palace. I've come here to make an offer of marriage. Open the gate quickly, I want to see the King," Even behind the walls of the palace his shouting sounded as loud as thunder and echoed in the ears of those inside for a long time. Shocked by the sound, the King and his ministers looked through the windows and saw it was a little frog making all the noise at the gate.

"Who are you?" the King asked. "Why are you shouting?"

"I'm the son of the old woman who carries water for the palace," the little frog said. "When she came to seek a match, you not only refused her, but were also very harsh with her. That was unfair! Yet I still respect you, and now I've come to see you myself. Will you agree to give me one of your daughters for my wife?"

The King roared with laughter and turned to the ministers at his side, "Did you hear what he said? The little frog dared to speak like that. How can such things happen?" Then he turned back to the frog, "How can my daughters, as lovely as flowers, be married to you, a dirty little thing like a cow pat? Scram! If you don't, I will set my dogs on you and they can eat you alive."

The little frog replied, "Don't try to frighten me. If you really won't grant my request, I'll start to laugh. Don't blame me for what happens then."

The King retorted, "Do as you like but don't complain of a belly ache if you laugh too hard!"

The little frog opened his mouth wide and laughed, letting out an enormous laugh. The sound was so loud that even the mountains and the earth shook, the wind blew, the sun and moon became dim, and the palace trembled as if about to collapse.

The King, scared out of his wits, popped his head out of the window and cried out, "Stop laughing! I'll go and find out which of my daughters would like to become your wife." The frog was silent and everything returned to normal. The King went inside and asked his eldest daughter first.

She replied, "Father, don't you love me any more? How could you propose marrying me to the son of that old woman? What's more, he's a small, dirty, ugly frog. I'd rather die than marry him!"

The King went back to the little frog and said, "My eldest daughter doesn't agree to marry such a small, dirty, ugly frog as you and your laughter was most unpleasant."

Before he could finish, the frog blew up his belly like a balloon and interrupted him with a loud cry, "What! If you won't let me marry one of your daughters, I'll weep!"

The King said, "Do as you like! Tears won't help you. My eldest daughter refused you, and I can do nothing about it. When a cow doesn't want to drink, you can't force it by pushing its head down."

Upon hearing this the little frog opened his mouth wide and cried. His tears poured down in torrents. Before long, the palace was flooded with water that continued to rise. Waves dashed turbulently against the walls and the palace seemed about to collapse.

The King, terror-stricken, begged at the top of his voice, "Do stop weeping! I'll go and ask again." This time the King went to his second daughter.

She replied with tears in her eyes, "Father, are you trying to get rid of me? If not, why ask me to marry the son of a servant?"

The King helplessly went back to the little frog and said, "Little frog, I was really unable to persuade my second daughter. She says you're the son of a servant, not a man but a frog, so she refuses to marry you."

The frog said, "You still don't want to give one of your daughters to me, so I'll jump up and down!"

"You have laughed and cried. You can do whatever you like!" the King retorted.

Then the little frog started jumping up and down more and more violently. With each jump a house collapsed under his feet and nearly all the houses around the palace caved in. Even the palace itself was rocking.

The King looked terrified and stammered, "Stop jumping and I'll give you my youngest daughter."

Young as she was, the third daughter was very clever. She said to her father, "He knows such powerful magic, I don't mind that he is the son of a servant. I'll marry this little frog, so long as you and mother and all the people in the palace can be saved."

Relieved, the King hurried outside, "This time your wish is granted," he announced to the little frog. "I'll let you marry my dearest daughter, the youngest princess."

The little frog was pleased and expressed his gratitude to the King. The young Princess was immediately dressed in her finery by her ladies-in-waiting, and the palace was gaily decorated. To the deafening sound of gongs and drums, the youngest Princess and the little frog were escorted home. Seeing that their sister had married the frog, the two elder sisters pouted and went back to the palace annoyed.

The old woman opened the door and found that the frog had really brought the Princess to be his wife. When the old woman asked him how he had managed to persuade the King and the Queen to give him the Princess, he told her how many times he had begged them and how many times he had been cheated. The old woman was overjoyed when she saw that the little frog had brought back the gentlest, most beautiful and virtuous daughter of the King. But then she began to worry when she thought about how poor her family was, with nowhere for the King's son-in-law and his bride to live. Without showing any signs of discomfort, the little Princess began right away to help the old woman: cleaning the house, carrying water, collecting cow pats for fuel and cooking. At night, the whole family slept together in one room.

The following morning, when the old woman woke up, she found that the poky, dark room they had been lying in had been transformed into a high, spacious building, bright and clean as if made of crystal. There was enough food, clothing and provisions for their daily needs, and their home was more comfortable even than the King's palace. Only then did the little frog tell the old woman and the young Princess his story.

He was the son of the old Dragon King of Dragon Kingdom and had come to the mortal world wearing a frog's skin. Then he removed the frog's skin and changed into a handsome prince. The old woman and the young Princess were so happy that they burst out laughing. Now the whole family could live comfortably, and there was no need for the old woman to work as a servant any more. Before long, the old man retuned home and they were all very happy.

One day, the young Princess suggested, "Why don't we invite my two sisters here? We don't need their favours, but we are related and we ought to show each other some affection?"

The Dragon Prince replied, "Your two sisters were cruel. We'd better not invite them."

But the young Princess insisted, so the Dragon Prince gave in on the condition that he should disguise himself as a frog in order that his secret should not be revealed to the two princesses.

The two sisters arrived. When they saw the big building and the many fine furnishings, which were better even than those of the palace, they were suspicious of the old woman's good fortune. At night when they drank barley wine, they made one toast after another to their youngest sister. As expected, the young Princess became intoxicated and talked so much that she disclosed the secret of the little frog.

Being jealous of her, the two sisters thought up a scheme. Unnoticed by the others, they threw her into a pool while she was drunk. Who would have thought that they would murder their own sister? Then the eldest Princess put on the fur gown of the youngest Princess and lay on the bed.

As the little frog went upstairs, the second Princess hurried towards him and said, "My elder sister has had to go back to the palace on some urgent business." The little frog did not bother to check this, though he wondered why she had left in such a hurry without saying goodbye to him. As the three sisters strongly resembled one another, it was hard for him to distinguish one from the other.

Time passed. A walnut tree grew out of the pool and bore many nuts. The little frog brought them back home and they tasted delicious to him and the old couple, but to the two sisters they were like a bitter poison. In anger, the two sisters chopped down the tree and burnt it to ashes, which were spread over the fields.

Later a lot of tender green barley sprouted up. When it was ripe, the little frog made it into *tsampa*. The old couple and the frog thought the *tsampa* tasted as sweet as honey, yet to the two sisters it was as bitter as medicinal herbs. Angrily, they threw all the barley into the pool, but it turned into larks, one of which flew towards the little frog and stood on his shoulder.

The little frog brought the lark into the house, and tearfully the bird told him how she had been killed. Only then did the little frog understand that the soul of his wife had been reincarnated as a bird. He drove the two evil sisters away, took off his frog skin and changed into young prince again. Then he and his family lived happily ever after.

she flew high above the clouds. They sang together and led a happy life, and it became even sweeter after they had three baby skylarks. But one day, the rain poured down and the water rose suddenly, so the whole valley was flooded. The three babies were washed away. In order to save them she and her husband jumped into the flood water and were drowned.

"Then they were reborn as thrushes singing and hopping joyfully in the trees all day long. They had some beautiful baby thrushes. They were very happy, and every day went to fetch food for their young ones. One day when they were out searching for food, a naughty shepherd boy was playing with fire and the nest with the little thrushes was burnt. She and her mate were so grief-stricken that they threw themselves into the flames.

"Then they were reincarnated as tigers and had two little cubs. One day some hunters shot all of them with arrows. She was then born again as a girl. She feels deep sorrow whenever she recalls her unhappy experiences as a skylark, a thrush and a tigress, so she believes that marriage is bitter and that happiness leads to misery. That's why she is so melancholic all the time, never speaks and ignores those who come to seek her hand."

Topgyal kept the old woman's words in mind, said goodbye to her and went into the valley. The girl saw another young man approaching and was sure he must be coming to propose. Disgusted, she shut and bolted the door. Topgyal pretended he hadn't seen this and walked slowly, speaking in a soft voice, "I learnt long ago that you lived here. I didn't come earlier because my family is poor. We both suffered the same cruel fate, so why do you hide when you see me?" Then he went on, "Don't you remember that we were both skylarks and happily spent days and nights together? Then all of a sudden, our babies were washed away by the flood. In trying to save them, we also perished."

The girl, standing inside the room, was shocked to hear these words. Opening the door, she went to sit behind a loom, as if about to start weaving, but still she remained silent. Topgyal noticed that his words had had some effect on her and so he walked over to the loom and continued, "Have you forgotten that we later changed into thrushes and thought that this time we would have a better life? But the unexpected happened. A shepherd boy set fire to our nest. Our babies died in the fire and we threw ourselves into the flames. Our happy life again came to an end."

The girl stopped weaving and listened to him attentively. Topgyal recounted his story, "I'm sure you haven't forgotten how we were born as tigers and had two cubs. Yet we were no luckier than before and were all killed by the hunters on the top of the mountain. Now you have been born into this family and I am suffering in a poor family at the foot of the mountain. I've come all this way only to tell you what happened to me after we parted. But it appears you've forgotten everything and even gone so far as to close the door in my face. I never expected this." He was so sad that he started crying.

The girl left the loom, her tears welling up. She grasped Topgyal's arms and said, "We'll never be parted from each other again. All this time, no matter who came to me, whether the son of a chief or the son of a rich man, I never said a word to them. I've been waiting for you alone."

To the great surprise of all the villagers, especially his two friends, Phuntsok and Wangdu, Topgyal married the girl soon afterwards. Phuntsog and Wangdu kept their promises, and gave half of their property to them. And so the couple lived happily ever after, the mute girl no longer troubled by her tragic past.

The Stone Lion that Opened its Mouth

Nobody remembers when this happened but it occured at the foot of a very old mountain. Only two men lived there. One was very rich and his name was Tenzin; the other was very poor and he was called Phurbu. Phurbu chopped firewood every day and made a living out of selling it. When he went up the mountain, he always took some *tsampa* for his lunch, so that he would be strong enough to chop more wood.

Nobody lived on this mountain, but there was one stone lion there. No one knew where it had come from or who had carved it on that mountain. Every day, when Phurbu had gathered a bundle of firewood, he would sit by the stone lion to have his lunch. And without fail, he would hold a lump of *pak* in front of the stone lion, saying, "Brother Lion, have some *tsampa*, please!" Then he would put it into the animal's mouth. He did this day after day, month after month, year after year.

One day he gave some *tsampa* to the stone lion as usual, but scarcely had he finished speaking when the beast opened its mouth and said, "Thank you, Brother Phurbu. You really are a kind-hearted man. Though you have very little to eat yourself, you're always willing to share it with me. How can I thank you?"

Phurbu was startled to hear the stone lion talking. Only when he realised it meant him no harm did he breathe more freely. Then he began to chat with it. "Brother Lion, we're in the same situation. You've nobody to take care of you, and we both suffer from loneliness. So it is natural for us to share the little I have. But it's a pity that I'm so poor that I will never have enough to satisfy your hunger."

The stone lion rcplied, "You really are an honest man. Please come here early tomorrow morning before the sun rises and bring a bag with you. I'll do you a favour." Phurbu agreed and went back home with his firewood.

Before dawn the next day, Phurbu, as usual, went up the mountain with his axe and a small bag of *tsampa.* He stopped in front of the stone lion and the latter greeted him, "So, you've come, brother."

Only then did Phurbu remember what the stone lion had said yesterday and replied, "Of course."

"Put your hand into my mouth when I open it, and you'll find some gold there. Please take as much as you can to fill your bag. But remember to withdraw your hand before the sun rises, for I'll close my mouth then."

"All right," Phurbu assured him.

As the stone lion opened its mouth, Phurbu rolled up his sleeves and put his hand inside. Sure enough, there was the gold, and before long the small bag was full. Phurbu then said, "Brother Lion, I'm so grateful to you!" The lion replied that he could have taken more if he had brought a bigger bag. Phurbu showed the lion his bag and said that it was enough to last a lifetime. At this moment the sun rose. The stone lion closed its mouth and lay there serenely. Phurbu then continued to cut wood and after he had collected a bundle, went home excited about his unexpectedly acquired wealth.

With the gold Phurbu bought some provisions, clothes and set up a courtyard home. He also married a nice, industrious girl. Now he did not have to worry about anything any more.

The rich man, Tenzin, did not fail to notice that Phurbu had become wealthy overnight. He thought to himself: That poor wretch did not own even a hair from an old donkey's hide, but now he has large flocks and herds and has also erected a high building with a storehouse of provisions. How did he come by these things, through cunning or robbery? Anyway, he would try to find out. Tenzin went to Phurbu's home as casually as if it was only to say hello. He began by saying many flattering words and then asked Phurbu how he had become so rich.

Phurbu was a simple man and very naive, so he told Tenzin the whole story in detail. When the latter heard it he felt so envious that he could hardly control himself. With a heavy sigh he groaned, "I've never encountered such good luck. Why couldn't I have had such good fortune?" He began to plan how he might avail himself of this opportunity to make a fortune. He asked Phurbu many questions: where the lion was, how to give it *tsampa*, how to cut firewood, even when one should go up the mountain and come down. He returned home only when he felt he had learnt everything.

That night Tenzin was too excited to sleep. The next day, he put on a worn-out sheepskin *chupa* and, carrying an axe, a rope and a bag of *tsampa*, he went up the mountain before dawn.

From that day, Tenzin kept on going up the mountain, sharing *tsampa* with the stone lion and speaking to it. Many days passed, but the stone lion still did not open its mouth. He grew anxious and wondered if he had been deceived, or whether the food he gave the stone lion was too little. In order to obtain the gold he persevered, and at last the moment came.

One day the stone lion spoke out, "Friend, you feed me every day. This'll be the last time I trouble you."

Tenzin was overjoyed at hearing the stone lion talk, so he said, "It is alright with me even though my family is very poor."

The stone lion continued, "Don't worry. Bring a bag with you tomorrow, and I'll give you something." When Tenzin heard the last sentence he became very excited and agreed without any hesitation.

The following day he got up very early and went to the lion with a very large bag. The lion warned him that he must withdraw his hand before the sun rose.

"Sure, sure!" Tenzin agreed impatiently, and asked the lion to open its mouth quickly. When the lion opened its mouth he pulled out one handful of gold after another.

The stone lion reminded him, "My friend, you have already taken so much, the sun is about to rise!"

Continuing to put gold into his bag, Tenzin declared that it would be full after a few more handfuls. But the bag was too big, and there was still some room left.

The lion again warned him, but he did not stop. When he put his hand into its mouth for the last time, the sun sprang up from the east, and hung over the mountain tops, shedding its rays in all directions, and dyeing everything red. The stone lion closed its mouth.

Unable to withdraw his hand, Tenzin started crying, "My hand! My hand!"

The Story of a Magic Treasure

Long ago in a remote place, there was a very greedy rich man named Wangden. Though he levied all sorts of taxes on the people throughout the year, he was still not satisfied. After the peasants had handed everything over to him, the only things they could call their own were their shadows and footprints. A peasant called Tsedub was so poor that he had to sell all he possessed in return for two pieces of woollen cloth. He put these on the back of his donkey and went off begging. Sorry to leave his home, he looked back over his shoulder every few steps.

One day he saw a group of children at the roadside playing with a mouse. They tied a string around its neck and threw it into the water. Then they pulled it out and threw it back many times until the mouse was almost dead. One child said, "Let's skin it alive!" The little mouse trembled when it heard this. The scene reminded Tsedub of how a rich man had made him suffer, and this aroused his pity for the little creature. He said to the children, "Hey kids! Why are you tormenting this little mouse?"

"None of your business!" one child shouted at him.

Tsedub said, "Well, shall we make a bargain? I'll give you this piece of woollen cloth for the mouse. What do you say?" They all agreed. Tsedub set the little mouse free afterwards.

Another day Tsedub saw some boys teasing a little monkey at a park along the road. They taught it various tricks, but if the little monkey failed to do them or did not perform well, they slapped it with a leather whip. The creature wriggled and cried. The scene made Tsedub recall how a tribal chief had tortured him and made him lose his teeth. Feeling pity for the monkey, he exchanged another piece of cloth for it and set it free in the forest.

Tsedub, leading the donkey, went on until he came to a crossroad in a village. He saw some hunters with a young bear which they were forcing to do tricks, much to the amusement of the onlookers. Seeing that the poor creature was suffering a lot, Tsedub thought of his own bitter life and asked the hunters, "What if I exchange my donkey for your little bear?" They agreed without hesitation. So the bear was set free in the forest too.

After that he had nothing left for himself. One night he arrived in Lhasa and stopped at the gate of an official family to beg for something to eat. But just at that moment a steward had stolen a package of embroidery from his master and was rushing towards the gate. It so happened that the mistress returned then too, and it was too late for the steward to hide. Suddenly the steward rolled his eyes and threw the package in front of Tsedub, crying, "Stop! Thief! Someone has stolen something!" Some ruffians appeared and nabbed Tsedub, who was taken before the master.

The master was furious. "You dare to steal my things! Put him into a hide bag and dump him into the river!" he ordered. As soon as the order was given, Tsedub was trussed up and put into the bag. After it was closed, he was thrown into the river that ran through Lhasa. The current carried the bag far away and it later became entangled in a tree root. Tsedub imagined he would be drowned very soon. He regretted begging at the gate of the official and hated the cruel man and his steward. It seemed that there was nothing he could do except wait for death.

At this moment, the mouse, whom he set free earlier, was searching for food by the riverside. It nibbled a hole in the hide bag and through the hole he saw Tsedub's eyes. The mouse quickly recognised that this was the man who had saved his life sometime back. He hurried back to the bank and called his friends. Both the little monkey and the bear appeared. They decided that they must rescue Tsedub. They tore open the bag with much effort and pulled him free. Then they asked him to sit on a log. They took turns at keeping watch, looking for food and scouting around. When it was the little bear's turn to scout, he saw something glittering nearby. When he went up to it, he saw that it was a magic treasure as big as a bird's egg. He brought it back to Tsedub.

Delighted, Tsedub prayed, "Treasure, treasure, please build me a three-storey building with furniture and food inside and a stable at the rear, a ballroom in front and a garden at the entrance with all kinds of fruit trees so that the four of us can lead a comfortable life."

Soon after this prayer, a spacious home and yard appeared, with all of the things he had asked for. He and his three friends moved into it.

One day, an old acquaintance of Tsedub, a businessman called Ralpachen came along. Seeing Tsedub living in such luxury, he thought: "He was a beggar. It was a struggle for him to make ends meet. Yet now he has built a mansion and lives well. How strange! There must be something more to it." He asked Tsedub time and again how it had happened. Tsedub was warm-hearted and very honest, so he told him the whole story without concealing anything.

Ralpachen was a very greedy person. He said to Tsedub, "Old friend, you have so much property, it's really marvellous. But what a hard life I'm living. Would you be so kind as to lend me your magic treasure so that I can have a try?"

Tsedub was a kind-hearted man, who would help others whenever he was asked. He gave the treasure to Ralpachen. The latter knelt down and prayed to it that very night, "Treasure, treasure, take away all the things from Tsedub and give them to me." The treasure ran about and took away whatever it saw until there was nothing left for Tsedub.

The next day when he woke up, Tsedub found the embroidered mattress he had been sleeping on had disappeared. Instead he was lying on the hard plank he had used in the past. He looked around and saw everything was gone. So he had to resume his begging.

One day when the bear, the monkey and the mouse came across their friend begging in the street, they went up to him and asked him what had happened. Tsedub told them the whole story.

The monkey was very angry and said, "Ralpachen is a wicked man. How can one drink another's buttered tea and offer cold water in return? The fellow's mouth is as slippery as butter and his heart is as vicious as blackthorn. Lets go and get the treasure back."

Ralpachen had built a large house, with one courtyard after another. After looking around for some time, the three friends still had not discovered which room was his. The little mouse, who could run very fast, found him snoring in a luxurious room with the treasure hanging from the head of a brightly-coloured arrow standing in a mound of grain. A cat was tied beside it, so the mouse dared not approach. He scurried out and told his two friends what he had seen.

The bear said, "We can do nothing. We'd better go back!" But the monkey said, "I have an idea. Tonight, let the little mouse go to Ralpachen and steal his pigtail." That night the mouse did what the monkey had suggested.

The next day when Ralpachen woke up, he found his hair lying scattered on the floor and cursed in anger, "My hair was chewed off by a mouse. If I'm not careful, perhaps he'll nibble the rest of my hair. You damned mouse! I'll put the cat at my side tonight and see whether you dare come again."

That night the bear and the monkey waited at the door. The mouse went into the room and found the cat no longer there. The treasure was still hanging from the arrow but the mouse couldn't climb up it, so he went back to his two friends. The bear felt they should leave as he had no idea what to do. But the monkey suggested that the mouse go and move the grain so the arrow would fall. The mouse went back to the room and did as the monkey said. The treasure fell to the floor. The mouse was pleased, but he was too small to pick it up, let alone move it. He came back again.

The bear, after hearing the mouse's report, lost heart and insisted on leaving. But the monkey told the mouse, "Tie a string to your tail. Then go and hold the treasure tightly with your four paws and don't move. We'll pull you out from here." The mouse went back with a string attached to his tail, and the treasure was hauled out at last. All of them were overjoyed at their success.

On the return journey, the monkey, with the treasure in his mouth, rode on the back of the bear. The mouse, having been busy all night, was very tired, so he climbed into the bear's ear and fell asleep. As they crossed a river, the bear thought: "I can carry the monkey, the mouse and the treasure, how great I am!" He asked proudly, "Am I very strong?"

The mouse did not reply, for he was sleeping. Neither did the monkey, as the treasure was in his mouth. The bear became angry and threatened, "If you two don't answer my question, I'll throw you into the river."

The monkey grew worried and opened his mouth, pleading, "Don't throw us into the river!" At that the treasure fell into the water.

After they reached the other side, the monkey complained about the bear, who had no idea how to retrieve the treasure and wanted to go home. The mouse asked them to think of a plan. Then he went to the bank and started running up and down. He seemed extremely agitated and cried out in a squeaky voice.

The fish, shrimps and frogs all asked, "Little mouse, why are you so upset?"

The mouse answered, "Haven't you heard that a group of soldiers who can fight both on land and in water will come here?"

The frog asked, "What can we do then?"

"Erect a wall at the banks to keep guard," the mouse proposed.

The fish, shrimps and frogs began to move the stones out of the river to the side and asked the mouse to build the wall. When the wall was about four or five inches high, a big frog with the treasure in his mouth came out of the water. "This stone is really heavy", he declared.

The bear and monkey went over to the frog and took the treasure away. The little monkey praised the mouse, "You're really smart." Then the monkey put the treasure in his mouth and rode on the back of the bear, while the little mouse got into one of the bear's ears again; The three friends returned to Tsedub, who was about to die of hunger.

He was so delighted when he saw the treasure, he cried, "Thank you, my three friends! He then prayed to the treasure. Soon, a building which was much more beautiful than the King's palace appeared, with as many fruit trees as in an orchard. Birds sang, and the air was sweetly scented. It was green all year round, and the friends had everything they wanted. So they lived happily ever after.

Glossary

Bo	— a Tibetan unit of measurement, probably equal to a bushel.
Bodhisattva	— Tibetan: Jan-chup Sem-pa, meaning the one who aspires to and is actually engaged in the path to Buddhahood for the sake of others.
Buddhadharma	— the Doctrine of Buddha.
Chang	— a favourite Tibetan brew similar to beer made only out of barley in Tibet, but now commonly made out of rice and wheat due to the difficulty of obtaining barley. Whatever it is made out of, it is still called chang. In the Tibetan folk tradition there is a whole philosophy surrounding chang.
Charu	— a thick coarse blanket, commonly made out of yak hair.
Chemar	— a ceremonial offering made of tsampa (see below for explanation) mixed with butter, raisins and sugar or jaggery (brown sugar). Chemar offered during Losar (Tibetan new year) is much more elaborate than those offered on other occasions. When offering chemar, chang must accompany it.
Chom-den-de, De-zhin Sheg-pa	— Bhagawan Buddha, the One thus gone.
Chupa	— a coat-like Tibetan gown worn by both sexes. Men's chupas differ slightly from those of women both in style and the way they are worn. Women's chupas have undergone a drastic change in style since 1959, in that they have become much easier to wear and also require less cloth. See illustration on page 136 for a man's chupa and page 3 for a woman's.

Demong	— a gorilla-like animal found in Tibet and the adjoining Himalayan regions. This is probably what some adventurers have called yeti, the abominable snow man.
Dharma	— the Doctrine of Buddha; it could also mean any religion when used in its context.
Doma	— a tiny vegetable-like a sweet-potato, found in abundance under the ground in Tibet. It is one of the main ingredients of an auspicious chemar.
Dri	— a cross between a yak and a cow. To an unaccustomed eye yak, dzo (seebelow) and dri might look alike.
Dzo	— a female yak, and as useful as a yak.
Ha'i-sing-pal	— a very special kind of flower. The word itself is probably Chinese.
Hor	— a tribe of nomads.
Jowo Rinpoche	— another name for Buddha Shakyamuni.
Karma	— the law of cause and effect of Buddhist philosophy. All happiness and good things that you enjoy in this life are because of merits accumulated in your past lives, and vice versa.
Lama	— traditionally used to describe a spiritually evolved being, but commonly applied to monks in general.
Lonpo	— a minister.
Mag-gam	— mag-battle; gam-box. This is a word created in the story having no specific reference to any commonly known thing.
Mantra	— a tantric recitation.
Mirgö	— a wild beast similar to a gorilla.
Nāgā	— the inhabitants of an underground kingdom often associated with serpents. Their Tibetan name is 'lu'.
Patuk	— a decorative Tibetan head-dress studded with coral, turquoise, ruby and gold. It may be round or triangular in shape. The opulence of its decoration shows the status of the woman wearing it.
Phorpa	— a Tibetan wooden cup. A woman's cup is slightly smaller than a man's and is also slightly different in shape.
Ribong	— a hare.

Rinpoche — 'Precious One'; commonly refers to a reincarnate lama.

Pak — kneaded tsampa dough is called pak.

Sang — a denomination of Tibetan currency.

Thangkuk — a small leather bag used for kneading tsampa dough It is common in every house but is also the trademark of beggars.

Torma — long cone-shaped religious cake.

Tsampa — powdered form of roasted barley; a staple food of the Tibetans. People nowadays make it out of roasted wheat and maize, but still call it tsampa.

Tsog — short cone-shaped religious cake.

Yak — an animal native to Tibet. It is a beast of burden renowned for its strength, stamina and surefootedness. Its meat is very tasty and its hide is very useful for making bags and drums. With its horns people make snuff cases and tool handles, etc. Its tail hair is very strong and makes good ropes and provides good strings for guitars and piwangs, an instrument like a lute.

Zongpon — district magistrate.